The Stone Harvest

Daniel D. Baumer

"Farewell happy fields, / Where joy forever dwells: hail, horrors, hail!"

John Milton's 'Paradise Lost'

1 - Tuesday

Spring 2019

The stones came up every year. They crept through the soil bit by bit with the annual frost heaves as the earth chilled and thawed. Oval stones that cost $200 per ton elsewhere would litter the land if left alone. This field had sat fallow long enough. Last year, my first on the property, I paid a neighbor to disc up the field and broadcast a native grass-and-seed mix: fescue and wildflowers. Ignored for several years, the twenty-acre patch had turned to non-native grasses, knapweed, vetch, tansy, and oxeye daisy. For nearly twenty years, no cattle had grazed, nor had anyone mowed or burned or sprayed. Nothing. It was perfect for the five-year project I had in mind.

The land was dead flat, a triangle whose eastern side ran northeast along what had once been a railroad line. Bordered by Wyoming Avenue to the south and with neighboring hay fields to the west, it had a drainage ditch between the two that was filled with the fruits of previous stone harvests. The field itself would still need a few more years to recover, but some carefully managed goat grazing, when I eventually get them, and harrowing should bring it back to its native condition. I had no desire to use the land for hay. Instead, I wanted to create a wild oasis, my very own

1

piece of somewhat controlled order in this world filled with so much uncontrolled chaos.

For the second time in as many springs, I rode an old tractor over every square inch of the field, dragging a harrow rake. The previous owner's family left the equipment behind when they abandoned the property, and I was more than happy to put it to good use. Harrowing knocked down any furrows caused by the discs, filled any low spots, and gave the seeds a good covering of earth in which to take root. It also taught me how many stones there were in this field. On many other properties nearby, I had seen huge piles and long rows of stones dumped after someone had harvested them. A farmer would work the soil, then send a son or daughter out with a pickup or four-wheeler and a trailer to collect them. The rock harvest would take longer than any other aspect of the farming cycle. Nothing was growing yet, and the kids needed a chore to keep them out of trouble. Hence, this part of the country had lots of fields with four-foot-tall stone walls bordering them.

It was during this, my second season of stone harvesting, that the problems began. The year before, I had noticed an unusually large collection of stones, or rather, so many in one tight place. It didn't seem like the rest of the field, but I didn't give it too much thought. There were plenty of stones to deal with, so there was no use getting worked up over these few. This year, the same problem in the same area. The harrow grabbed enough of the buried nuggets that it dislodged the others, exposing ten or twelve to the gray sky. It was unusual enough to get on my radar, but not enough to alter my plans.

I didn't return to that spot for two days. Harvesting from other parts of the field, I already had an impressive collection for the stone wall I hoped to build. By the time I returned, sure enough, the rocks hadn't moved on their own like I had wanted them to. One by one, they went into the back of my new-to-me farm truck.

BAM!

BAM!

The low clouds and the closeness of the mountains made the din of granite on metal echo loudly—a rich, satisfying tone.

The effort of moving the stones left me with a modest sweat, but the chilling breeze worked just as hard to cool me back down. As I cleared the first few stones, I could see several more an inch or two below the surface. *Might as well,* I thought. There was no way this project would be easy, so I kept plugging along. By about the twentieth stone, I ignored a growing suspicion that the rocks were in an unnaturally neat, elongated shape.

"Nope. Perfectly natural." I half-whispered to no one in particular.

It was the thirty-seventh rock that did the trick. Nothing special about it. Mostly gray, a few black specks, and two white ribbons going through the center. Its uniqueness lay beneath it. I saw the cuff of a sleeve, remnants of what was probably a gray hoodie or sweater. And with it, a small, desiccated hand.

Though not a surprise, I had to take a step back to collect my thoughts. It's not every day that you find a dead body. Rarer still to find an old one buried on your property, property you bought and moved to for the direct purpose of not finding dead bodies anymore.

Despite the apparent age of the body and its long-term exposure to the elements, it still had traces of that smell, that goddamn smell of death and decay.

I said to the world my first clear words of the day, "Well … fuck!"

2

Chief Christian Sanchez sat at her desk, reviewing personnel records. She had come in earlier than usual to weed through the files and work on a few of the department's longstanding staffing issues. Though she'd been in the role for over three years, the city manager still kept her on a short leash when it came to bringing in new blood to the department, especially when it came to culling the deadwood from the team. That needed to change, but it wasn't going to happen anytime soon. She had barely spread the files out on her desk when she got the call from Warren and had to catch the newly found dead body. She stacked them again and secured the lot in her right-hand desk drawer.

The chief didn't like dead bodies any more than any other cop. In fact, the fewer dead people she had to deal with, the better. Not at all an unusual point of view. This part of the country had plenty of ways to create dead bodies, whether or not anyone wanted them. Sometimes it's the environment. Sometimes it's a farming accident; sometimes it's sheer stupidity, or the evil humans can inflict on each other.

When Sanchez left Kansas City, Missouri, she expected the amount of pain and misery she encountered to diminish. This had not been the case. Having a corpse found on Warren's property, while unsettling, wasn't that much of a shock. Sanchez gave up being surprised about such things a long time ago.

"Hannah!" the chief called to the clerk on duty, then grabbed her black wool cap. "I'm headed out on a call. Your boy Karl Warren found a dead body on his property. Lord knows that man can make trouble if he can't find it. I'll call dispatch and let them know."

"The Baker place?" Hannah said it more like a statement than a question. Her cold tone stopped the chief in her tracks.

"Yeah. Why? You know where he lives."

"Well," the desk agent looked down at her desktop, and a lock of her blonde hair fell forward, covering part of her face, "it's probably nothing. It's from before your time." Hannah looked back squarely at her boss, her hands lightly gripping the edge of her desk. "When Charles Baker died a few years ago, well, that's when the girls stopped disappearing. Maybe it was just a coincidence, but there were a few of us who always thought there was something more to it."

The chief said nothing, knowing this wrinkle required more time and mental bandwidth than she had at the moment. She made her exit.

Sanchez took the department's blue-and-white Ford Explorer and weaved through a couple of blocks of Westwood's old residential neighborhoods to Highway 41. Two miles south of town, she got on the first of the gravel roads that would lead to Warren's lonely home on the prairie.

The chief and Warren had known each other for many years, since Kansas City, since the academy, where a younger Sergeant Sanchez was an instructor, and Cadet Warren was a new boot fresh out of the Army. Their first interactions were neither warm nor friendly, largely because of Warren's youth and arrogance. Sanchez gave him plenty of rope, recognizing that his post-military vigilance and refusal to accept traditional rules of civilian behavior made him slightly harder to mold than the other recruits. She had spent ten years in the service herself, in the Air Force, and she knew how hard that transition could be. When Sanchez's days at the academy were over, and she was assigned to the same patrol division as Warren, two years into his tenure with KCPD, they became tight friends.

After too many murdered children and dead bodies bloated from the Missouri heat, after one breakup too many, Sanchez had had enough and, on a half-calculated whim, applied for the position of Police Chief in Westwood, Idaho. The job was what she was looking for, and they were looking for someone like her—new blood. Sanchez had read all about the missing women. The lack of closure on their cases was a stain on the town, and the last chief, and the stench of that affair is part of why they hired someone from outside the state.

Two years later, she was pleasantly surprised when she got a call from her former patrol mate asking for help in setting up a soft landing place in her quiet town. What were the odds that Warren would be the guy to find a dead body on his property? Pretty good, actually. If anyone could find trouble, it was he.

Before he had moved into the place, she hadn't visited the property but had driven past it a few times, always noting the impressive collection of old car and truck carcasses. The overgrown weeds were a nice touch, she had thought. The previous owner had been dead for a few years, and the home had stood abandoned until Warren moved in. She recalled how quickly he had gotten rid of the vehicles. As she pulled closer, she saw that the front area was still a mess of weeds, but it was coming along nicely.

Warren was on his front porch, sipping coffee, when she pulled her vehicle into his front lot. The image she saw was nothing like the doorkicker she had known back in the day: flannel shirt, jeans, sitting calmly surrounded by a few of his hens.

"Morning, Chief. Cuppa?" he said, raising his mug.

"Maybe in a few. Let me see what you got, okay?" she replied more coolly.

"Can do." Warren got up and walked around the east side of his light blue pole barn of a house while the hens and the chief followed. "I told you a couple of days ago that I was gonna spend some time harrowing the field and collecting the new stone harvest. I was working on a thick patch of them this morning and found a new friend."

Sanchez noted that one thing about Warren hadn't changed. He still walked too damn fast. It wasn't only that, she thought. It was in his shifting gears so quickly. It took her twenty-five strides to catch up to him and match his quick, martial pace across his field of stubble and dead grasses. Warming up, she took off her wool cap, letting her short, dark hair catch the Idaho sky. The spot where they eventually stopped was twenty-five feet away from the modest rock pile that Warren pointed toward and 200 yards north of the barn wall. Warren

8

stayed where he was, but after a pause, the chief understood and proceeded alone. She knew Warren had also moved up here to get away from dead bodies and was reluctant to spend any more time with them than he had to.

As she got closer, it was easy to see which way the stone grave cover was oriented. The few rocks covering the body's hands had been removed, exposing part of her abdomen, a gray sweater, and about six inches of her forearms.

Sanchez looked toward Warren, pointed at the body with her wool cap, and asked, "Did you try to give CPR?"

Back in the day, Warren had always been the one with a quick bit of gallows humor. She tested out the line, not so much as a cheap joke but to gauge where her old friend's mind was.

Nothing. Just a cool stare in return.

She got up, dusted herself off, and headed back to him. "I'll take that cuppa now if you don't mind."

3

Fall, 12 years earlier

"Look," Tracy told Barry outside in the mill's log yard after their shift. A cold mist was lifting, and the nearby mountains were showing through the low clouds. "Just meet me there. I'll show you the copies, and we can figure out how to handle this. This is our way outta here. We don't need much. Just enough for a new start somewhere. You can divorce your cow of a wife, leave her that shitty trailer, and we can get the fuck out of here."

Tracy Goodson knew what she wanted out of life. Unfortunately, none of those things existed in Kootenai County, so she did the best she could with what she had. What she had was just enough to get her in trouble: poor parents, good looks, and bad choices in men.

Twenty-four years old, living in a trailer park in Athol, and dating a married coworker from Upriver Mill. Her youth and looks gave her a shot at life, but the trailer park and mill life doomed her to an existence far less than she ever imagined. Her boyfriend, Barry Gillum, was fun company, but she knew well enough that it wasn't true love. There was a part of her that hoped, though.

"I've been here long enough to know what's going on. I've seen all the reports. The real ones and the fake ones. If this stuff gets out, Mallard is fucked."

She had access to the company's reports on its discharges into local waterways. She had seen the raw data and the second, falsified report sent to the EPA. If they had been dumping as much filth into the Belmont River as she thought, the result would be an environmental disaster.

Her concern wasn't about the wildlife in the area. She thought getting copies of the real and the false reports would be a great bargaining chip to secure a payoff to keep her mouth shut. She had an instinct for self-serving acts but no clue how to proceed. She wanted to talk to someone about it. Unfortunately for her, that someone was Barry.

"Let's talk more at The Snoot, not here. But really, you don't want to do this," Barry protested feebly. "He's not gonna let it happen. You know full well that Mallard will do whatever it takes to stay outta trouble. "Barry placed his hands in front of him in a prayer position, looked straight into her eyes, and spoke slowly. "This is a bad idea, and it's not gonna end well."

Tracy was not impressed by his words and steamrolled right over them, jabbing her outstretched finger into his chest. "You just be there at eight! Why do I have to be the only one in this relationship with a set of balls?" she said. It came out as a half-whisper, half-hiss, the way mothers talk to their children in public, right before they deliver a spanking if they don't behave. She turned and walked away without waiting for a response.

* * *

Barry Gillum stood stunned. She was right. He didn't have the nerve for this sort of thing, for

11

blackmailing the boss. Crossing Gerald Mallard was not a good idea. On top of all that, he really didn't want to run away with this woman. Yes, he hated his wife, and she hated him, but he sure wasn't ready to leave on a moment's notice like this. He was with Tracy for a bit of fun, and he may have developed some soft feelings for her, but in her desire to escape and start a new life, her dreams and emotions had spun a fantasy and a plan of action all on their own.

After she walked away, he stood in place for a solid minute, thinking about how to handle this mess. As usual, he had no idea what to do in cases like this except to talk to Cha about it. *That ol' fucker will know what to do,* he thought.

Barry entered the same admin building as Tracy had, but through the entrance inside the mill. Cha's office was down the hallway from Mallard's. The boss always wanted to keep Cha within yelling distance whenever a problem needed solving. That's what Cha was now—a problem solver. Production problems? Cha could deal with it. Labor shortage? Cha could fill every role in the operation that needed filling, either by himself or by one of the many men he knew in the area who were always looking for work. A manager gets caught with blow or a hooker? Cha found a way to smooth it over with the deputies or Staties. Money or blackmail usually worked.

* * *

When Gillum entered, Cha was seated on the couch in the corner of the office, next to the coffee pot.

12

Cha's slight frame and slicked-back hair made him look even older than his fifty-plus years. Though his right hand was empty, he held it up as if he were holding a lit cigarette—an old habit.

The office was an interior one, with no windows. The paneling was the same fake wood that had been there since the factory was built in 1968, and the furniture didn't seem much newer. Though the space was nowhere near stylish, Cha was such a meticulous cleaner that the water-and-vinegar mixture he used to clean the place had almost masked the smell of decades' worth of cigarette smoke.

His doctor ordered him to stop smoking the year before. Though he was never one to take advice from anyone, Cha had coughed up enough blood in the previous months to think long and hard about that piece of wisdom. Between the menthol cigarettes and the chemicals at the factory, Cha figured he'd listen this time. So, he stopped smoking cold turkey and never thought twice about lighting up again.

The office was sparse. The heavily worn tan carpet held an old metal desk near the far wall, accompanied by a metal filing cabinet to the right. On the desk, a computer sat unused. A painful reminder that times were changing, times that Cha didn't want. In the corner to the left of the door lay the old teak-and-leather sofa, chair, and table that had sat there for nearly 40 years. This was where Cha held court. In all the times he'd been in the office, Gillum couldn't recall ever seeing Cha at the desk. This was where business was done, next to the coffee pot.

"We have a problem!" Gillum blurted. He had given a courtesy knock but still half barged into the office. Cha sat in his corner like a spider waiting for a fly, seeming to know that something was about to happen. Maybe he always wanted problems to occur, so he always stayed primed for action. Gillum told the story of Tracy's plan as best he could, and Cha listened, eyes soft, but the wheels in his head were turning.

"Okay. I got this," Cha spat.

"You gonna tell the boss? This is gonna be a mess," Gillum whined.

Cha took a moment, leaned forward, and stared hard at the kid. "I got this. What time are you supposed to meet? Eight? Pick me up at my place at six forty-five. Don't say a word about this to anyone. Keep the meeting as planned and play nice. I got this."

He leaned back in his chair and looked straight ahead into the room. He repeated himself for good measure. "I got this."

* * *

Barry had known Cha long enough to notice when an emotion surfaced. Cha always kept a calm demeanor, especially in his vampire mode, as he sat in his dimly lit office. It was no different as he recounted his story about Tracy. Still, near the end, when Cha had to decide, Barry saw a flicker in his eyes, a hint of excitement. Was it stress or worry about the blackmail? No, he'd seen Cha stressed before, and it didn't look like this. Cha seemed to be looking forward to it, excited about what was coming.

14

The ride from Westwood to Blanchard was uneventful. Late in fall, before the snow began in earnest, all the seasonal residents had departed, and no one was playing tourist in these northern backwoods. The sun had already started to go down, and the close mountain range to the west blocked any of the slivers of the setting sun from lighting up the woods here. The headlights of Gillum's truck were the only thing bringing light to Highway 41.

Cha sat in noticeable silence, and Barry knew better than to ask questions when the old man was in this state. He wanted to know what would happen, but he was too worried about upsetting him and drawing his ire. He knew he was partially responsible for this mess, so it was best to keep his mouth shut as much as possible.

* * *

The Snoot was an old tavern near Blanchard, tucked away from the highway and barely visible behind the natural hedge of alder saplings, hawthorn, and ninebark. Were it not for the neon lights on the place, passersby in the dark could easily miss it.

"Park in the back," Cha said calmly. There were two other trucks in the front lot, but only one in the rear, larger lot, probably belonging to Rob, the bartender.

"Park there!" he said as he pointed to a space in the gravel darker than the rest of the area. When they stopped, Cha said, "Give me your phone and go in and wait an hour. Tell Rob that you're waiting for Tracy. Watch TV, drink a few beers, keep your mouth shut about anything else. Your phone will be here in your seat when you come back."

Barry sat stunned for a minute, staring blankly at Cha. The old man looked calm, yet he still had an air of excitement and animation he'd never seen before. "Give me your fucking phone and get the fuck out!" Cha said more forcefully.

Charles "Cha" Baker hadn't gotten his hands dirty with floor work at the mill for several years. Back in his working days, he had started as a bleacher, one of the workers responsible for soaking the milled pulp with the toxic array of chemicals needed to make it usable down the road in the paper mills. Cha started at a mill up north on Highway 2 near Bonners Ferry when he was sixteen and has been in the industry ever since. He wasn't afraid of hard work, but he was always smart enough to find a shortcut when it worked out well enough. Over the years, he hadn't been afraid to push out a competitor or supervisor to get a promotion or a raise if the opportunity presented itself. Over those same years, he had gone through three wives and three children, to whom he never paid much attention. Cha was not someone who anyone would call lovable.

With phone in hand and the kid out of the way, Cha went to work. It was 7:40. Early, but who knew if Tracy would be on time or not? With his heavy coat on, Cha slipped out of the cab of his truck, shutting the door with as little noise as possible, and walked about 100 feet into the woods to the west of the lot. He grabbed a seat on a downed log and pulled Gillum's Razr phone out.

HERE EARLY. PARK IN BACK.
NEXT TO MY TRUCK.

Cha texted like Gillum would, all caps and curt language. Cha rarely said much, but he appreciated the English language more than the kid did. He also knew that cell service between Spirit Lake and Blanchard was spotty, so she might not even get the text.

Ten minutes went by. The woods were dark and quiet, echoing his mood. A car came from the north, parked in the front lot, and then all was quiet again. More witnesses to see Gillum sitting alone inside the bar. *Good.*

Ten more minutes. The Razr vibrated with a new text from Tracy.

K

That was all it said. Cha wanted to know her ETA but decided not to press the issue further. He saw the headlights and outline of her car appear moments later as she came close to The Snoot. She had done what he had asked. She pulled into the lot and chose a spot near the truck. It wasn't as close as he had wanted, but it'll do. Before she had even entirely entered the lot, he had moved from his spot in the woods toward her, left hand in the pocket of his green Army coat that he'd had forever.

He did his best to keep a tree between him and Tracy as she pulled her car the last few feet into her spot, and when he got to the edge of the clearing, he waited. He was behind a thick Douglas fir about twenty feet from the car, and to her nine o'clock. Inside the car, she looked as if she were fixing her makeup for the last time before seeing Barry. *For the last time ever, if I could do this right.*

She finished her touching-up and opened her door. Cha moved. He moved toward her in an arc that brought him behind her as she put one foot out of the vehicle and started to stand. When he was ten feet away, he got his left hand out of the pocket of his coat and pointed his Taser gun at the exposed flesh around her neck. Just as she stood on both feet, she turned around, and both electrodes stuck into the flesh of her face, one on the left cheek and the other into the softness of her neck. She didn't have any chance to react, and she slumped to the ground, spasming as the voltage ran through her slight frame. Cha kept the trigger pulled for a few more seconds to ensure the shock was complete.

Moving quickly, he pulled the electrodes out, wound the fifteen-foot-long wires around the gun, and shoved the whole thing back into his pocket. He pulled out a pair of zip cuffs, secured Tracy's hands behind her, opened the rear door, grabbed her, and tossed her into the backseat with the strength and ardor of a younger, stronger, bigger man.

He grabbed her car keys from the gravel, where they had dropped after the initial attack. Moving over to Barry's truck, he opened the driver's door gently and set the kid's phone onto the seat. He shut the door as quietly as he had opened it and, after a final look around, got into Tracy's small car. He slowly exited the lot, took a right turn onto 41, and was lost in the dark Idaho night.

The back of The Snoot had no windows, nor did the south side, where Tracy entered the lot, so it was likely no one saw her car when it arrived. If they had, they would also have seen her car leave a minute later.

* * *

Inside, 'Hold on Loosely' by .38 Special was playing on the jukebox while Gillum worked on his third Kokanee, waiting for the girl who would never come.

4

The fishing boat captain was almost home from the sea. Escorted by a cohort of seagulls that rode the wind and swooped in the air currents to steal loose fish from the nets, he and his men had been in the Gulf of Alaska for nearly two weeks. As much as he loved the water, he wanted to be on land again, with his wife and close to the bars. Their hold was full of herring, and it had been so for almost two days. He was ready to return home when he got the call on the radio to pick up one more load. This load wasn't more fish, though. He wasn't sure what it was, and he knew better than to ask. The voice on the radio was unfamiliar, but he would be paid well enough not to ask that, either.

The accented voice gave him specific coordinates nearly forty miles west of Baranof Island, where he was to await further instructions. After waiting eight hours, the next call sent him to another set of coordinates, where a buoy waited. Attached to it would be a floating, sealed bundle that he'd treat like a sack of newborn babies swimming in mother's milk if he knew what was good for him. This was his fourth trip like this in as many months, so he and his crew knew what was expected: do everything as asked and get paid handsomely. Fail, and he'd be killed. Simple as that. The Ukrainian "family" that helped him get his fishing boat had certain expectations of him, and he understood what was at stake.

The captain suspected the delay was because of the weather. When he got the first call, the tail end of a high-pressure system was passing through the eastern part of the gulf and was making the chop more than any skipper would like. By the time the second call came, sending him south, the sea was as close to glass as it was going to get.

Using the expensive, accurate navigation gear the "family" had provided, he headed toward the second destination. He slowed his boat, *The Odessa Princess*, and came alongside the bright orange buoy. One of his deckhands used a gaff pole to grab the float by its rope. Getting the package onboard was challenging, but no more so than a net full of herring. *As long as the damn thing was on the boat and secured, and we don't lose any men or fingers.*

His hold was full, the bundle was on board, his men were safe, and they were headed back home. Another smooth transfer lay ahead, and he would be free of obligation until the next time. The bundles awaited their journey across Canada and their visit to an Idaho lumberyard that had seen much better years.

5

The chief texted me

You busy?

Yes. Very.

GFY! Come to the station.

10-4! Gimme 30.

After the chief's team had left, I returned the tractor to the barn. I needed to run the harrow over the burial site a few times to smooth out the soil again, but I didn't have the stomach for it today. Instead, I went to work on tearing out the broken and worn slats of the old shelter inside the goat pen. There were no goats yet, but the plan was to bring in a few to roam the field and graze down the weeds.

The shelter was cobbled together from a wide variety of random bits of lumber. It looked horrible, but it had a sturdy frame. Five feet tall in front, it sloped downward for ten feet. The opening was three feet tall, and I had to stoop and crawl to get inside. One corner needed bracing, but otherwise, I just needed to replace some siding, and the goats would have a cozy place for most of the year. Come the depths of winter, I could move the whole shed into the barn and fence off a small area for them to weather the worst of the ice, wind, and snow.

I had torn off a broken panel when the chief texted. As much as I appreciated the solitude of life on the prairie, I did want to escape the farm now and then. Also, the idea of sniffing around a case like this gave me a slight thrill. I put the broken slats on the burn pile and returned the tools to the one neat corner of the barn where I'd begun to carve out some order in an otherwise chaotic mess.

After a quick shower, I grabbed two dozen eggs from this morning's gathering and headed out on my way in the Honda CR-V, the same one I'd had in Kansas City, the same one that Laura helped me pick out. She talked me out of the truck I wanted by selling me on the Honda's sensible, practical city use—and maybe even hinting at space for a car seat in the back. It seemed a thousand years ago. I had purchased a farm truck soon after moving here, but it was a workhorse, better suited to trips to the landfill or the lumber mill. Not for a social call.

Wyoming Avenue was a gravel road that led to another road, which led to another road, which led to the heart of downtown Westwood. My place wasn't remote, but it was on the flattest part of the Rathdrum Prairie in this area and at the furthest reach of Westwood city limits. Most of northern Idaho was mountains, lakes, and rivers, except for richly soiled valleys like the one I lived in. The valley was one of the most fertile areas in the Inland Northwest, and in a few weeks, farmers would be in full motion, trying to squeeze in at least two crops of hay and straw. Three, if the weather cooperates.

Part of the acreage was directly underneath the power lines that cut a swath across the outer territory of the city and county. As I made my way, the circuitous route to town brought me beneath the lines twice, and each time, if the radio were off and the windows down, I could feel and hear the electric sizzle in the air, the tens of thousands of volts hanging in the wind. The towers that held the cables were massive, engineered to bear the tons of steel as the wicked, seasonal winds blew. As their lengths get pummeled by ice, snow, and hail through the winters, they hold. Every year. Quiet, steady strength unconcerned with receiving gratitude. Their sole purpose, to further modern life.

The Westwood Police Department's headquarters was next to the town's sole hotel and one of its two bars. Most businesses on this stretch of Main Street were closed except for the small engine repair shop and the daycare center. The center's playground was a patchwork of chipped plastic and rusty metal. A tetanus farm, basically.

I grabbed one of the visitor spots and entered the station from the sidewalk. Its foyer was a white box, twelve feet by twelve feet, all stucco, plexiglass, and old magazines. The receptionist, City Clerk II Hannah Gustavson, was on duty and immediately buzzed me in.

"Here ya go, Hannah!" I said, placing the egg cases on her desk.

"Thank you, Karl! The boys and I always love the eggs," she said coolly—but with a hint of hope.

24

Hannah needed only the horned helmet to meet Wagner's vision of Scandinavian perfection. She was 40, blonde, tall, and stout in all the strong, warrioress ways. Twice-divorced from men who didn't deserve her and with two sons who looked as if they had futures in the NFL. In another time and place, she and I might have been a perfect match—but not in this world. After a brief flirtation shortly after I got into town, I knew it wouldn't work. The ghosts wouldn't allow it, so I backed off, leaving Hannah to wonder what had happened. The eggs were part of my compensation package for her.

Once past the security door, I entered a great room that served as a shared office for the patrol officers and the lone detective. Along the far wall were offices for two administrative staff and a bigger, glass-walled office in the most distant corner. This was where the chief's office was. A hallway led past her door to a modest detention area, one interview room, and a secure evidence storage area.

Sanchez was waiting for me behind her desk, with the latest reports and photos from my field in front of her. On the credenza beside her desk, I saw where she hoarded my coffee mugs. The chief always had a cuppa when she visited, and she often left with a mug in her hand. This is where they lived until I visited and retrieved them.

She looked healthy. I hadn't noticed it this morning as I was too focused on the dead girl in my dirt, but this job has been good for Sanchez. Leaner, stress gone from her face, better color. Sure, some gray was coming into her short, dark hair, but she had found a sense of peace up here that she didn't have back in Missouri. The streets and her divorce had gotten to her. I knew that stress, and I knew that peace—until a few hours ago.

"Good morning," she said with fake cheeriness. "Wanna see what we found?"

"No, thank you," I blurted. I'd already seen the body in the dirt and added it to the already extensive catalog of death images in my memory. Now that I was here, I realized I wanted to be part of this investigation less than I'd thought. "What do you know about the girl or how she was killed?"

"We don't yet know who she is, but Oliveira is putting together a list of missing girls who match her description and the time frame she was buried. We'll know more after the autopsy."

"Cause of death?"

I was all business now, a defense mechanism. Classic avoidance, and I knew it.

"Looks like either blunt force trauma to the head or strangulation. There's evidence of both, plus lots of other physical abuse, but we'll know more later."

Williamson caught her eye when he walked past her door with a fresh cup of coffee. "Hey! Will," she said. "Come in for a sec."

"Chief." He stepped in, and I made way for the old cop. "What's up?" He nodded at me. "How's life as a chicken rancher?" I didn't take the bait. I just smiled.

Sergeant Quinton "Quint" Williamson was an imposing figure on the streets, even more so up close. On the downside of his fifties, his face showed evidence of his many years living and working in the extreme weather of Northern Idaho.

"Take a look at these pics of the gal we dug up at Warren's place. Imagine ten to fifteen years back. Does she strike you as familiar in any way?"

He grabbed the photos Sanchez handed him and leafed through them without expression. One of them was an unflattering, up-close shot that, despite the years of deterioration in the earth, clearly showed what her face might have looked like. A trace of red revealed what her final choice of lipstick color was, and the one earring in her right ear hinted at the stylish vanity of the dead girl. It was a hoop earring with a tree symbol at its center. I couldn't help but steal a glance at the image while Williamson surveyed the badly decayed face.

"This was not a boating accident," he said plainly. "No, ma'am. Not a bit. Oliviera getting a list together?"

"Yeah. She's on it right now."

"Let me take a look at it when she's done. It may jog a memory," he said before heading out the door.

Williamson was the longest-tenured officer on the force, with almost twenty-seven years now, but he didn't start his adult life as a cop. His family had been in the area for several generations, and all had worked in the timber industry in one way or another. He had distant kin at almost all the mills in Montana, northern Idaho, and northeastern Washington, as well as dozens of relatives crisscrossing the Inland Northwest as rig drivers. The few family members who didn't fit those categories spent time in the woods with the teams, harvesting trees for processing and shipping across the country.

The old cop excused himself to finish an accident report. His 250-pound frame barely fit through the shared space. At six feet three inches, Williamson was all muscle and gristle. Once at the desk and in the chair, he reached into the cargo pocket of his dark blue tactical pants and grabbed his phone. He hastily typed a quick message before shoving his phone back into his pocket.

6

15 years earlier

Sergeant Warren, U.S. Army Military Police, wasn't crazy about Fort Jackson, South Carolina, but he loved the graveyard shift. It was mostly quiet, and there were plenty of opportunities to explore every square inch of the basic training post, becoming familiar with every building, practice area, and barracks compound. It wasn't the real patrol work he had hoped for when he received his transfer order here. Despite that, he enjoyed gaining an intimate understanding of the fort, its inhabitants, its pace, and its character by roaming its lonely miles. The weather was always hot and humid, and the bugs were big and plentiful.

Warren was on foot patrol in the administrative center near Gate #3. This was the gate where most of the troublemakers would try to sneak in and cause havoc on base with petty crimes, and where the teenage Army brats would come and go with their civilian friends. It was mostly quiet, but on many nights, he found someone slinking around who shouldn't be there. Often, a call to his civilian counterparts at the Forest Acres Police Department would do the trick. If Warren had to file paperwork for a misbehaving soldier, it usually meant the end of a career, so he tried to avoid that unless it was a serious offense. He'd made several informal calls to duty officers or noncommissioned officers to get soldiers off the streets and out of sight.

In-house punishments were undesirable but preferable to an other-than-honorable discharge.

"Base to 4-3," came a call from Dispatch.

"4-3, go!" replied Warren.

"Respond to a call about a suspicious Ford Bronco parked near Bynum Pond, one-quarter mile past the turnoff to Training Area Gallup. The reporting party is a Hispanic male, age twenty-three, in a two-thousand-one Ford Mustang. Last name, Ramirez."

He'd been out to Bynum Pond several times before, mostly for basic security checks, but sometimes to shoo off young lovers. *If you're out there*, Warren thought, *you're probably already in trouble. That's where folks go when they're with someone they shouldn't be with. This Ramirez guy obviously didn't know that.*

It took seven minutes to reach the scene from where Warren had initially received the call near Victory Tower. He notified dispatch of his arrival, pulled in, and parked his patrol car with the nose barely left of center relative to Ramirez's vehicle. His headlights bathed the Mustang in bright light, and Warren turned on the spotlight on his light bar and the movable spotlight on his driver's side door—this one he aimed directly at the Bronco. Right away, he saw what Ramirez saw, and the moment he opened his door, he smelled what Ramirez smelled.

Within three minutes, Warren had called for backup and a crime scene team from CID, the Criminal Investigation Division, and had sent Ramirez down the road a quarter mile to meet up with PFC Dornan at the intersection with Dixie Road. It had taken Warren sixty seconds on-scene and a chat with Ramirez to figure out why the kid was out there and that he was no threat.

Abraham Ramirez and a young trainee had driven along the back roads of Fort Jackson seeking a bit of peace away from the post and all the officers and NCOs. He was a young specialist stationed with a training battalion, and she was an even younger private, a trainee in the same battalion. They chose a small turnout off the road near one of the many little training areas they both knew, having passed the road on many trips by bus and cattle car to and from a rifle range, a Nuclear-Biological-Chemical center, or a Field Training Exercise site. This little spot near Bynum Creek seemed like the perfect location to get to know each other better.

When Ramirez made a sharp turn into the almost hidden place, his headlights swept across the body of the white Ford Bronco tucked away near a copse of evergreens and on the downward slope toward the small pond. Right away, even in the brief time that the headlights passed over the driver's seat, he could tell that something wasn't right. There was a man slumped over the wheel.

Ramirez backed his car up so the lights would rest on the Bronco's cab. As he reached under his seat for his personal weapon, a Taurus 9mm, which was modelled on the Beretta he'd been trained to use and had used in Iraq, he instructed the already scared young Private to stay where she was and not to make a sound.

He could smell that unique scent of death the moment he opened his door, and as he approached the vehicle, he stopped twenty feet away. The stench of decay was too fierce. He returned to his car and made the 911 call on his cell phone. Ramirez knew he would get into trouble for taking one of the young gals out for fun, but he made the call anyway. Hopefully, his commander considered that when deciding on his Article 15 punishment. Dornan took Ramirez's complete statement.

For now, Warren was alone with yet another dead body until his patrol supervisor and squad leader, Staff Sergeant Walker, arrived. He was speeding in from the station and would be another few minutes. As Ramirez left, Warren grabbed the small jar of Vicks VapoRub from his go bag and smeared some on his upper lip. The menthol scent helped—but not enough.

At about twenty feet out, he walked two concentric circles around the Bronco, the second one tighter than the first. He didn't see any obvious threat or disturbance. That was all he was willing to do until the Suits from CID arrived. They didn't even wear suits, so he wasn't sure why they were called that. Polo shirts were their usual attire, but "the Polos" didn't sound right. After completing the second lap, Warren came to rest beside the driver's door and shone his light into the cab of the SUV. The driver was in his combat uniform, slumped against the wheel. His hands were out of sight, and his forehead rested on the steering wheel. No one and nothing else of note appeared to be inside the cab. While not a trained crime scene investigator, Warren assumed the problem had something to do with the large-caliber exit wound in the back of the man's skull.

At the start of the shift, SSG Walker had told them to be on the lookout for a missing soldier, SGT Antonio Muscatelli. He's been missing since a fight with his wife. Warren and his patrol mates assumed the sergeant had finally found out that his wife had cheated on him while deployed to the desert, a sadly common occurrence.

SSG Walker arrived fifteen minutes later, but it wasn't for another hour, as the sunlight was beginning its rise, that the Suits showed up. Warren was supposed to be End-of-Watch by 7 am, but this was his case to catch and complete, so it would be a long morning. The Suits snapped photos of the area and the vehicle from every angle.

Suit #1 noticed the hole in the vehicle's roof and made a quiet comment to Suit #2, "There's gonna be maggots."

At this point, there was nothing else to do except open the driver's door. Immediately after the investigator released the latch, and the door cracked open, a wave of stench roared from the vehicle, and there wasn't enough VapoRub to mask it. With the door fully open, the heat and vomit-inducing stink came out in a rush that filled the surrounding air—both Warren and Suit #2 retched and puked. Suit #1 and SSG Walker seemed barely bothered by it.

"Yep. There's maggots," said Suit #1 as if he were reading a restaurant menu.

Had the good sergeant used a smaller caliber handgun, there might not have been as big a mess as there was. In addition to making a bigger opening in the back of his head, the .45 Automatic Colt Pistol sent its round clean through Muscatelli's head and out the roof of the car. Had it not been for that, the flies and other insects might not have made their way inside the cab.

The jagged hole was plenty enough space for all manner of South Carolina's six- and eight-legged residents to enter, feed, and find space to lay their eggs. SGT Muscatelli was very generous in that regard, in that there were easily a hundred insects of several species feeding, breeding, fighting, and fucking on every square inch of his exposed flesh.

"Here comes the fun part," said Suit #1 as he reached for Muscatelli's left shoulder to pull him back from the steering wheel. He didn't move easily, though. In the several days he'd been there, the raw flesh and gore on Muscatelli's face became one with the leather steering wheel cover, and he didn't seem to want to go, to be exposed in the new insult. Suit #1 adjusted his grip and his stance, gave a stronger pull, and …

7 - Wednesday

That's where it always ended. Since that day, I hadn't been able to picture what Muscatelli's face looked like when they pulled him back upright in his seat. I remembered the smell. I remembered assisting with evidence collection. I remembered the tactile sensations of hefting the man's weight from the seat onto a stretcher. I remembered the smell.

I remembered the smell.

The bed was warm; the rest of the world was cold, and I didn't have the energy to get up. I didn't have the energy to fight the world anymore, nor did I have the energy to handle any more hate. Then Big Red, my lone rooster, began his morning ruckus. I smiled and figured that at least I had enough energy to take care of the flock.

The night was all fitful sleep, and the memories of the dear departed Muscatelli didn't help much at all. I moved up here to avoid death and misery, but it had now visited me here, on my piece of paradise, my homestead. Over the years, I'd found that the salve for a night full of demons and mind-monkeys flinging shit was a peaceful morning with a pot of coffee. Now, with the new land and openness, I'd been able to add a new element to my mornings. Chickens.

I had never raised them before. Despite growing up in Missouri, we weren't that kind of family. I hadn't even considered raising them when I moved up here, but after a few weeks in the place, Sanchez asked me to foster a few that had been left behind when a local resident had passed.

"You've got the space, and you certainly have nothing else going on," the chief had said.

So, I became the guardian of three Ameraucanas, three Rhode Island Reds, and a handful of mixed bantams that started fighting each other the moment they arrived and hadn't stopped since.

All hens, save one. Big Red. Big Red was a Rhode Island Red and perhaps the biggest chicken I'd ever seen. Keep in mind that at this point, my experience with live poultry was limited to seeing them at state and county fairs. Apparently, the previous owner bought a batch of chicks the previous season, and this one was a misfire, a male. The chick sellers are generally effective at separating the males, but Big Red slipped through their system. As soon as he arrived here, he was King! The hens all gave way to him when he came around, and even the neighbor's goat learned the hard way about who ran the place when she escaped her pen on the neighboring property and came over to explore my recycling bin.

During their time here, the girls did a fantastic job providing eggs, but the first few weeks were rough. Some girls went missing. I'd thought we'd lost a couple to predators, but they had been brooding their clutches in different spots inside the barn and in the abandoned goat pen. Within two months of getting the birds, the flock of a dozen more than tripled as all the different groups of chicks hatched. Since then, I have been meticulous about gathering all the eggs daily and ensuring that all the gals returned to the coop every night.

As the coffee brewed, I let the girls out of their coop and scattered their feed into the compost box. The box was eight feet by eight feet, two feet high, and placed about fifty feet east of their coop. I'd put it on top of a piece of ground I wanted to use as a flower bed the following season, so I would put the girls to work. In that box would go all the kitchen scraps and compostable food waste, as well as clippings and trimmings from around the yard. Even without putting the feed in there, the hens would be in and out all day long, scratching and turning it all in their hunt for bugs and mice. Their nitrogen-rich waste made a great additive to the composting process, and after about a month, I could flip the box to a new spot and rake up the big pieces that remained, adding them back to the box. I would use a spade to turn up the now-healthier soil and leave it fallow until needed. The box in its new space was ready for the next 64 square feet of chicken-powered magic.

I've never been a coffee snob. Any of the big brands would do if they were of a rich enough blend. With as much cream and sugar as I add, good coffee would be wasted anyway. Sitting on the porch, sipping whatever was on sale, and watching the sun come up over the eastern side of the Rathdrum Prairie was a cure for almost anything that ailed me. It was indeed the best aspect of my escape here. The screams faded, the smells dissipated, and the visions grew dim. In the distance, a tractor was already working in a neighboring field, preparing the soil for planting. This tiny slice of the world was perfect for this moment of life.

I knew to savor these moments because, even if they return with the next sunrise or pot of coffee, magical moments fade. Sometimes slowly, and other times lightning-fast, but they do fade. The demise of this morning's peace came from a not-uncommon source: Laura, my lost love. She wasn't lost. I knew exactly where she was. What was lost was the love, faith, passion, and compassion we had shared for many years. Maybe lost wasn't the right word, either. Smashed, destroyed, wasted, squandered, and poisoned would all be adequate replacements, but I went with lost. Without her, I felt homeless because the only "home" that I ever wanted lay in her eyes. Those eyes looked elsewhere now and held no warmth for me. Everything else was a consolation prize: efforts to bandage the pain and loss from a mortal wound.

On paper, we had a great life. We had love, as we defined it, two significant incomes, no kids to squander it on, and a modest loft in the Crossroads, Kansas City's art neighborhood. We were fit, active people who shared a love of adventure and exploration of the wider world. We were perfect! On paper.

I met her at the wedding of mutual friends, which we had each attended with a plus-one. My date was a gal who loved the thrill of dating cops. Pretty, but just another pretty gal in a long line of equally pretty but empty partners. She was nice, but not nearly nice enough. Laura had gone there with a safe date. A friend and occasional lover who could watch her back if needed or be sent away if she wanted.

A stray glance turned into steady eye contact, which turned into a smile. That led to an intentionally random meeting at the open bar. I said nothing to her as we moved up to the crowded rail, sharing space but not words. We waited our turns, asked for our beverages, inhaled each other, created fantasies, forged futures, and then—she walked away.

I watched her as she did so, hoping she would turn around for a moment. She never did. Instead, with her free hand, she reached down to the table on her left side, extended her forefinger, and drew a delicate line through the pile of confetti that was gathered there.

The confetti was shiny, capturing every last ray of light in the wedding tent. In that glitter, or rather in its absence, I could see the line that she had drawn, wavy but still direct enough to point toward where my future had gone—a strong trail to follow.

Standing with two drinks in my hands, I had to choose: return to my date with them, or follow the new path laid before me.

I chose the new path to her. To Laura.

8

Sanchez helped me find this place. The previous owner, Charles Baker, died five years ago in an auto accident, and he did so without a proper will. His estranged children wanted nothing to do with Westwood or their dead father, so I hired an agent to buy the place for cheap at the county tax auction. I told Sanchez that I cashed out part of my retirement for it—a poor decision, in her opinion.

There was only one building on the land, a huge metal pole barn with a two-bedroom home attached to the southern side. I moved onto the farm at the beginning of winter, but as it was a mild one, I survived it easily enough. For the first two months, my home was a trailer that I rented and had delivered while the renovations were underway. I needed that time because the place was a mess. Abandoned for several years, it appeared someone had squatted in the residential portion for a while, leaving squalor behind. There were hints of black mold, too, so it was better to tear it down to the studs and start all over.

I'm good with a hammer, but I know my limitations. The demolition part was easy enough, but I brought in some professional contractors to handle the electrical work and all the new plumbing. I could have managed it in time, but the work would have taken three times as long, and I'm sure I would have overlooked a few things an experienced eye would have caught. Within three months, I had a whole new home. Modern yet still spartan, sealed tight against the worst winter could throw at it.

The faded blue pole barn was a gold mine I'd barely begun to dig through. The previous owner had owned the place for almost thirty years and seemed never to have thrown away anything with any life left in it. Tools with broken handles, implements for tractors he didn't have, engines without cars, trucks without engines, the stripped body of an old panel van suspended on cedar rounds, gear for horses he never owned, and all manner of nuts, bolts, screws, and random scraps of hardware that may or may not have ever had a purpose. It was 120 feet long, and the west and east-facing sides were eighty feet. The west side of the building had a twenty-foot-high rolling door and a personnel door beside it. On the east were two doors that swung outward and another personnel door leading to the chicken coop. That had a doggy-door flap and connected to a small pen, enclosed on all sides. Chicken netting covered the pen's top so the girls could play safely outside without the worry of a swooping raptor. The coop, which I had initially thought to tear out, had become the best thing about the entire property.

With so much square footage inside the barn, even with the previous owner's junk still there, there was plenty of available space. In the northwest corner was a small, enclosed office. It had little in it, but it was well made, essentially a small cabin nestled inside the larger space. It was so well insulated that even during the worst of that first winter, a small space heater kept the place warm enough to use as a warming hut while I did my winter chores. This space seemed to have been cleared out near the time of the previous owner's death. There was an empty desk, two empty shelves, and several empty cardboard boxes, but nothing of note. Not a single scrap of paper, photograph, or personal memento. The view from the window was epic. It faced true north, and I couldn't see a single home, farm, or barn. Just prairie and the distant forest on the side of Rathdrum Mountain. It would make an excellent office space if I went that route.

Stacked up in the corner that was formed by the barn's walls and that of the office cabin were dozens of boxes of all different sizes. These were the focus of my attention this morning. After enjoying coffee, watching the girls in their morning frolic, and getting dressed, I headed out to the barn with the plan to separate the contents of the boxes into different categories: trash, salvage, recycle, or sell.

I already had an impressive pile of scrap metal near the front edge of the property where it met the road, but I knew that the pile would grow until I cleared the old items from the barn. I'd made a burn pile, too. There were plenty of pieces of old lumber around and inside the barn, plus what looked to be four cords of well-aged red and white fir. So well-aged, in fact, that most of it seemed to have rotted away past the point of being any good for the wood stove. An outdoor bonfire would be the best use of it all, and the clean paper and scrap wood would burn just as smoothly. It will all be an excellent winter pyre in a few months.

The first four boxes all had receipts dating back twenty-plus years. Receipts for a grand variety of tools, seeds, implements, and fuel; handwritten invoices from the people the previous owner would bring on to mow, bale, or disk the field when he couldn't do it himself. Twenty-plus years of clean paper that would soon enjoy a fiery passing from this world to the next when the time came. Four larger boxes sat near the base of the pile. These contained an assortment of supplies and tools for the animals that probably never lived here: water bottles for various cages and hutches, small straps and harnesses for goats that have been gone forever, leaders and leashes for who knows what, mostly empty bags of pine shavings and alfalfa pellets, never-opened insect traps, and bird feeders, as well as what once was a beautiful ceramic hummingbird feeder, now cracked into two pieces.

One box near the base contained lengths of 20-gauge wire in various colors, including red, yellow, and bare copper. Some were half-empty spools, while others were pieces no longer than eight feet long. Some were untouched, while others had been used and then returned to storage. The box to its left held never-used, brand-new wooden replacement handles for hammers or hatchets. I assumed Baker had gotten a good deal by purchasing them in bulk. The box to the right of the wires held a jumble of paper scraps. I set that aside for later sorting, then turned my attention to the box behind it, the one with the wires. It lay buried beneath other boxes, but this one caught my eye because of the copious amount of tape sealing it.

I moved the other, covering boxes to the side for the moment, and grabbed the tape-covered one. It was an old banker's box with a faux-wood finish, as if that would make it look classier when in the storage room of a high-end law firm or financial office. The box was much lighter than the others and survived the weight of the ones on top of it because it was shorter than its neighbors. They bore the weight while this one hid peacefully at the bottom of the pile. I pulled it out, set it on the gravel floor of the barn, and, in one smooth motion, reached down, pulled, and unsheathed the four-inch lock blade Gerber knife that lived clipped to my right front jeans pocket. The old and dried packaging tape gave way easily to the blade as I quickly cut around the lid's base and removed it. With another smooth motion, I activated the thumb lock, closed the blade, then returned it to the pocket it had come from, tossing the box lid aside.

I knelt and saw that the contents were clearly not farm-related. An old baseball cap, a pair of terry cloth wristbands, a small white V-neck T-shirt, a pair of women's sunglasses with one lens missing, a pair of cheap smartphone earphones, one pair of green-and-white flip-flop sandals, a thin black sweater, and snagged on the left cuff of the sweater, a hoop earring about one inch in diameter with what appeared to be the outline of a tree and its roots in the center.

Not two earrings. One. An ornament that looked exactly like the one found in the hole in my field a day earlier. Precisely like the earring attached to the dead girl who had been living in my field for the past dozen or so years.

At times like this, if you listen closely enough to the human brain, you can hear the wheels of its machinery turning furiously. When presented with new data that matches old data, lines get drawn. A problem arises when the new conclusion is one the brain doesn't wish to accept. Then you may slip into denial or excuse-making. Apparently, I'd been out of the denial and rationalization game long enough that I couldn't make excuses quickly enough, so the new data hit me hard. I knew all too quickly and was all too sure what this meant.

My knees went wobbly, so I looked for a seat. A few feet away, an old truck engine lay near the outer wall. I reached for it and sat upright against the barn's support beam. I knew what I needed to do.

Just breathe.

No, more than that. I had to count them. It didn't matter how many it took. I had to calm myself and not let the ghosts take over. A department therapist taught me a simple trick to clear my head in times like this, and while it hadn't always worked, not doing it always promised poor results.

All I had to do was count each cycle of breath and feel the sensations in my nostrils as I did so. If a stray thought came in, such as the image of a dead girl in my field, I'd shift my mind back to counting. Sometimes, I could go as many as two breaths without thinking about the ghosts, but the victory wasn't in how long one could go without those bad thoughts. The victory came in acknowledging that right now, in this instance, everything is fine. All that exists is breath and life. It usually took about thirty breaths for me to calm my heart rate and reclaim my focus. I didn't feel magically reborn or washed in Zen-like calmness now. Still, the exercise reminded me that, at the moment, I was fine.

I stood up, looked at the earring in the box again, and wondered how many of the choices that I've made in my life up to this point have truly been in my best interest. All the horrible things I've done and lived through, all of my bad behavior, have apparently led to more of the same.

I could cover the box and toss it into the burn pile. That way, I could go on with my day and enjoy the warm sun as it lit up my chilly dirt. A bad thing happened, but it's over now, right? The dead don't care. They're not crying for justice. I came here to escape from this part of the world, and there's no reason to jump back into it.

You see and do enough bad things, and it hurts your heart. Other men and women I've known had seen and done far more than I ever had, and they seemed to have come out fine. They're still working patrol or moving on with their lives. Why can't I? Why did I feel the need to run away and escape? I can't figure it out.

Big Red had come over to see what the commotion was all about. Anytime there was a new movement in the yard or barn, if he were around, he'd come to make sure that all was in order and that his girls were okay. This time, though, he found a bonus. He was poking around where the boxes had been, and I saw him race to the back of the pile and reach his long, feathered neck in between two boxes. When he pulled out, I noticed he had caught a fat mouse, but Big Red didn't look pleased or relaxed about it. He seemed almost afraid, not of the mouse but of the two hens that saw him with the mouse. They stared at him. He stared back at them, but no one moved.

On an unspoken yet coordinated command, the two hens raced toward Big Red. He took off from behind the boxes and ran in a wide circle around the two girls while arching his way toward the door. Once there, other hens sensed the commotion and saw the treat that he carried. The race was on. I didn't go outside to watch because I'd already seen this play out a few times. One of the hens would eventually wrest the mouse away from the rooster, only for it to be stolen again and again. Sometimes the mouse would get torn in two, doubling the fights. The winner was the chicken that could run and swallow half a mouse simultaneously.

It was entertaining to watch the girls follow their dinosaur instincts. Gruesome as all hell for the mouse, though. I looked back at the boxes of souvenirs and remembered my dinosaur instincts. The dead may not care, but the living might. I remembered another thing, too, something one of my training officers told me: When there's one, there's two. Where there's two, there's more. He was talking about deer on the side of the highway, or bad guys with guns, or any number of threats a cop could face, but the rule applied here.

With a sigh, I went over to my tractor and lowered the teeth of the spike-toothed harrow to their maximum depth, about four inches deeper than they had been. She started up easily enough, so I raised the implement arm, backed out of the open rolling door on the west side of the barn, and headed to the south-easternmost corner of the field. A ten-foot strip between the field and the fence alongside the old goat pen gave enough room to bring the tractor in and turn north along the eastern edge of the former hayfield. I lowered the arm and etched the harrow into the earth on the first pass through the field. The teeth, now set more deeply than the day before, tore into the soil and grass, leaving ugly trails behind. My master plan for the field was to let the native grasses grow and form a robust, healthy seal on the land. Yet here I was, cutting deeply into it, tearing up the roots and leaving ugly, straight slashes in my land. I could almost imagine the soil bleeding out of the new wounds.

Every few feet, one or two teeth would snag on one of the hundreds of hidden stones, bringing it closer to the surface. Some I sensed through the shake of the metal, but others I saw as the rake exposed them from their beds: one here, two there, but nothing of note on my first trip up the field. I turned around at the tip of the field's triangle and headed back on a path that overlapped the previous pass by about a foot. The eight-foot-wide harrow rake was a great tool. Still, it would take a while to cover the entire field. Since I started with the longest edge, each subsequent pass would be a few feet shorter. Again, the large rake would shudder with each stone snagged, but the second pass bore no great fruit.

The year before I met Laura, I dated a statistician. She worked for one of the big financial firms in KC, helping them with various algorithms they used in their trading software. On one of our few dates, we were sitting at an outdoor table at Harry's Country Club in the River Market. She made a comment I didn't quite understand at the time, and I didn't appreciate it until now.

"Prime numbers are awesome!" she said with more excitement than anyone should have for numbers, prime or otherwise. "They're strong and powerful, and entire systems can be built around them, but because of that power, they'll always be troublesome. They'll be fine, but around them, you will always find glitches."

I smiled and nodded, trying to appreciate the words but really hoping the date would end at her place. It didn't.

On the seventh pass over the field, I found a glitch. I had begun to feel that all this effort would be for nothing, and that my imagination had gotten the better of me. I hated being right. *Where there's one, there's two.*

The teeth of the harrow grabbed a handful of stones. I had dislodged them enough to bring them to the surface, and the vibration from metal on stone carried through the tractor arm and up to me. It rattled my gut because I knew exactly what that sensation meant. I stopped the tractor a few feet past where the stones exited the ground, grabbed the hand mattock from the tool basket, got down, and headed toward the dark patch of soil. Maybe the earth only seemed darker because I knew what lay ahead.

I knelt near the stones and pulled up the loose rocks. Once those had been cleared and set aside, I used the toothed side of the hand mattock to probe the soil for more stones. I found them. They moved easily as I edged the teeth into the earth and pulled. More stones came up as I worked a four-square-foot area, gently but still with enough force to dive deeper. When I had loosened enough earth and stones, I grabbed them one by one and tossed them aside.

"Seventeen, eighteen, nineteen ..." I counted quietly to no one.

The twenty-third stone; another prime number. Once I moved, I saw what looked like a thin cotton-polyester blend coat in the empty space. Probably yellow when it came out of the clothing factory, now faded to a tan or off-white. The line of the zipper seemed to come or go directly away from me, which meant that I was kneeling either on her groin or on her head. Neither was a respectful option, so I stepped aside before continuing the work. I removed another seven stones and exposed more of her torso. Though there were no direct signs of identity or gender, I knew it was a "she." It had to be.

I had done enough. At that point, anything more might damage the scene, so I stood up, walked back to the tractor, grabbed my phone, and snapped a quick picture. I added it to the text that I sent to the chief.

Found another one! Better bring your guys out again.

Within a minute, I saw the bubble icon working and, soon after, the response.

Be there in 10!

9

11 years earlier

State Highway 53 ran from the Washington border near Otis Orchards through Westwood, crossing State Highway 41 near the center of town. There, it turned eastward, and 41 became the primary route north to Spirit Lake, Blanchard, and eventually to Oldtown. Along the way, the road ran through a desolate stretch and a few towns. Villages, really. It was a beautiful drive by day, but dark and lonely at night or any time in winter. In the thirty-two miles from Westwood to the Priest River, there were easily a hundred unmarked turnoffs that led to logging sites, remote homes, hunting camps, backwood trails, or abandoned sites that no one could recall anymore. Along this long span, you wouldn't find a streetlight, and rarely would you see any vehicles after dark.

This is where Karen's car decided to break down. She wanted it to last one more year or at least through one more winter. She had to get out of small-town Idaho, and she had a plan to do it. A bright, pretty twenty-three-year-old bartender in a county full of truckers and loggers could do well for herself if she wanted, but she didn't want that. Staying in her parents' empty cabin to save on rent money, she needed a few more months to save up for a newer car, travel expenses, and a little extra to soften her landing in her dream city, San Antonio.

Her parents took her there when she was fourteen for her older brother's graduation from Air Force Basic Training. It was twenty-two degrees and blowing icy snow when they left Spokane, and seventy-eight degrees and sunny when they landed in Texas. This was her first trip out of the Pacific Northwest, and she was giddy that she didn't have to wear her coat for the entire four days there. In her free time, she wandered the streets of downtown and walked every mile along the city's iconic River Walk she could. So much life and color in the dead of winter. It was then, at that young age, that she fell in love with San Antonio.

She would never live to see the town again.

* * *

Charles Baker was returning from a late night of drinking at The Snoot when he spotted a car facing northbound with its flashing hazard lights by the side of the road. He saw the young female driver standing near her car and knew an opportunity when he saw it: opportunity plus resources plus mood. Cha was not going to pass up this chance for fun.

He slowed down almost to a stop before he made a wide turn using the full width of the road. He kept his lights on as he parked facing the rear of Karen's car on the northbound side of 41. Before getting out, he reached into the van's glove box, grabbed his Taser, his newest toy, and pressed the battery-test button. Four lights. All was well.

He got out and strolled toward her, staying silhouetted by his headlights. He didn't say a word, and she didn't see what was in his hand as he raised it.

In the dim light, it seemed she recognized her Samaritan. "Oh, wow! Thanks for stopping. Aren't you—" she managed before the two prongs of the Taser struck her face.

Not perfect contact, but enough to complete the electrical circuit. From his left pocket, Cha pulled out his stun gun and applied it to the thin denim on her right hip. A few seconds of contact was all it took for her to lose motor control and fall into a heap.

He replaced the stun gun in his pocket, wound up the wire leads from the Taser, placed it into his right pocket, and went to clear the back of his van. Through one opened door, he moved two empty boxes out of the way and grabbed the blue tarp wadded in the corner. Returning to Karen's limp body, he grabbed her hands, dragged her to the back of the van, and opened both doors. After opening them, he straddled her chest, grabbed her heavy winter coat with two hands, and heaved her upper half into the open door. The way he rolled her legs in and over her head was downright disrespectful, but had to be done quickly. He grabbed zip cuffs from under his seat and returned to tie her and make sure that the blue tarp covered her for the ride home.

Cha loved winter. Sure, it was pretty, but he liked it mostly because those around him were too soft to go out into the cold unless they had to. The harsh climate kept the weak away from him and gave him ample room to do the things he loved to do: hunt, hike, fish, and find women to kill.

With his package bundled safely, the ride back to his place was uneventful. As he waited at one of the town's two stoplights at the northern intersection of highways 41 and 53, the girl stirred under the tarp. He grabbed his stun gun in case she needed another jolt.

No more sound. Another ten minutes and he was home. He pulled his van around to the western side of his pole barn, got out, opened the rolling door, and backed his van halfway inside. Cha threw open the van's back doors and saw the girl stir again. Not wanting to take a chance, he gave her a five-second-long taste of the stun gun. That calmed her down, leaving her limp again. Showing no hint of tenderness, he grabbed her ankles and, in one swift motion, pulled her out of the van, letting her fall harshly to the gravel and dirt floor of the barn. He threw the blue tarp aside and surveyed his toy for a moment, planning his next move.

His plan to get horses never panned out, but he had all the gear ready if he ever did. Moving briskly to the northeast corner where the tack room would eventually go, Cha rummaged through a pile of leather straps until he found the one he wanted: one inch wide, eighteen inches long, and with a solid buckle. From a pile next to it, he grabbed a longer length of hemp rope.

Returning to Karen, he placed the strap around her head and made sure it was seated firmly in her mouth before cinching the buckle on the back of her head. "There!" he said aloud. "That's for in case you got something smart to say."

Cha grabbed the shoulders of her heavy coat and dragged her limp body closer to where the stalls would be. In their construction, he had only gotten as far as partially framing the outer wall and installing the massive header to support the heavy gates. Attached to the header, Baker had already prepared what he needed: a solid length of chain with a carabiner.

Karen was stirring, so Baker used her energy by forcing her to stand. He could have muscled the girl up, but instead employed her wriggling to shift her upright. Once up on her feet, Baker replaced the zip cuffs by binding her wrists with the hemp rope, but after getting the rope tied, he left the zip cuffs as they were. From here, hooking the carabiner to the rope around her wrists was a simple task. With a minor adjustment to the length of the chain that he had used to bind her, Baker enjoyed the moment. Now he could take his time.

He took a few minutes to get his van fully inside the barn, grabbed the stun gun, and secured the door again. After he got the lights on the way he wanted, Cha strode over to the ancient potbellied woodstove near the corner where he'd be working and lit a mix of old paper, hay, and kindling. The warmth and glow of the growing fire helped calm the old man and gave him a moment to savor his work so far and what lay ahead. Baker added a few smaller pieces of split pine to get a quick flash and a few pieces of tamarack for a longer, deeper fire.

He sat watching the flames dance and thought of moments of happiness from his life around a fire: camping or burning slash piles with his grandfather. Times before his mother died. Times before his father climbed into a bottle and stayed there. Times before the beatings and humiliation.

Karen stirred awake and drew Baker's attention back to today, to now. He went back to her and gave her one more quick jolt on her thigh to keep her still for another few minutes. She had said something as he approached, but he didn't listen. There was no need to speak or listen anymore tonight.

With a smooth motion, he withdrew the knife from his front pocket and cut her sweater open. The first pass cut through her sweater and shirt quickly enough and exposed her bra and chest to the still chilly air of the barn, but Baker didn't stop there. He used the knife to cut a path along the sleeves of both arms, getting enough started that he could rip most of it away. The seams around the wrists were tougher, so he used the knife on them again. Her sneakers came off easily, as did her loose jeans.

Taking a step back to admire his work, Baker recalled the girl from the bar she had worked at near Hauser, a sometimes-loud honky-tonk that was quiet most weekdays. He liked the bar but not the people who went there. He knew most of them but hated casual conversations with anyone, even those he liked. When he went, he always tried to sit near the fireplace and enjoyed nothing more than sitting, sipping, and watching the flames dance. Cha couldn't recall if he'd ever spoken to her before tonight, but this was his last chance to do so.

He had tossed her clothing aside as he was disrobing her. As he moved close to collect them, she became fully alert and instinctively moved away, but she couldn't get far. Baker gathered up all the clothes and stuffed them into the stove piece by piece. He was worried that the metal eyelets of her sneakers wouldn't melt, but he could deal with that later. Everything else would burn and disappear.

Ignoring the girl for another few moments, he went to his office space and grabbed an item from behind the door. It was a four-foot-long fiberglass rod used to support the thin wires of portable electric fencing. He still didn't have the goats or lambs he had long intended to get, but he had all the gear. It was the second such rod that he had gone through. They're tough to break, but one time a year back, he had aimed a blow poorly, and it snapped on the hip bone of a previous guest. Since then, he'd learned where to strike and how hard. A learned skill.

The lighting inside had been bright enough for him to do what preparations he needed, but now that they were ready, he turned off all the lights save the one above the chicken coop. As he stood before the girl, he knew he was backlit, yet the stove's light cast a warm orange glow on his face. Baker allowed himself a moment to enjoy the theatrics and watched the gagged girl writhe in fear.

"I want you to know a few things," he began. "I'm not gonna rape you. I'm not gonna tell you stories about my mother. I'm not gonna want to hear you scream. In fact, I don't want anything from you. All you have to do is stand there until I'm done with you."

Karen was near-naked and afraid, but now confused, too. Baker continued, "What I am gonna do is strangle the life out of you, but before then I'm gonna take this rod and, uh, as they say, spoil the child." He knew he was warping that axiom; even so, he enjoyed the dramatic flair of it.

As much as one could scream with a leather strap cinched in their mouth, Karen screamed. A scream like she had never done before. Again and again, she screamed, but outside, the winter winds blew south from Canada, down the valley, and across the Rathdrum Prairie, washing over anything Karen had to say. To the world, she was already dead. Baker was going to make sure of that.

10

The county crime scene team came and went within a few hours. They performed the same operation on this new girl as they had on the last. They photographed the body from all angles, then turned slightly to search it and the grave for any artifacts or evidence that might have fallen loose. After placing a white sheet beside the hole, three pairs of hands lifted the girl's remains out and placed them on the sheet. They carefully wrapped the sheet around her, put her inside a body bag, and moved her again onto a waiting stretcher. Two team members carried her to the van, secured it, and returned to the grave.

Over the course of an hour, they sifted through the soil around the hole, searching for any additional items. Altogether, they went through about four cubic yards of soil in their hunt but found nothing new. I made a mental note of all the stones that they had dislodged. Discovering dead bodies proved a great way to get stone-free soil.

I didn't pay much attention to the goings-on as they unfolded. I'd check the scene now and then as I was going about my chores. Mainly, I finished up the work on the goat pen. I removed all the old slats and braced the roof-support corners with angle iron. It would be stronger than needed, but with all the snow that would come in winter, a few bucks' worth of iron was a cheap investment that would keep the roof from getting crushed. Also, last fall, the winds were strong enough to lift the entire structure and toss it, bottom-up, 100 feet into the next field. That's what had broken most of the slats and almost cracked the entire thing in half.

Within the first hour of the CS team's work, I had placed the new siding onto the goat shed and laid the new plywood on the roof. Over the second hour, the new aluminum roofing was in place, and I'd gone back over every square foot to make certain I secured everything. Drywall screws were cheap and would hold together long enough for my needs. In the third hour, I lifted one side of the shed at a time and shoved two cedar rounds under each side to lift the whole thing off the ground.

With all four sides suspended, I went around it and applied two solid coats of white paint to the exposed wood. The paint was an inexpensive blend I got in five-gallon buckets from Habitat for Humanity. They collected all the donated unused paint, strained it, blended it, and added pigments to create their own line: blue, green, white, and tan. Suitable for indoor and outdoor use. Perfect for goat sheds. I chose green. I like green.

I was finished almost at the same time the team was wrapping up their soil-sifting. The chief had long cleared the scene but had stayed in contact with the team at the farm. A minute or two had passed after the team had driven away in their white van when Sanchez called.

"They're all done. You can have your dirt back," she said.

"Thanks! Do you know who she is yet?"

"No," Sanchez replied, "but Olivera has narrowed down the list of Missings some more. Looks like she has similar marks to the other gal—lots of soft tissue damage on her face, neck, wrists, buttocks, and thighs. Nothing broken, but she was thrown around pretty well. No signs of movement once she went into the hole, so she must have been dead or unconscious when she went in. Poor thing was well and truly fucked!"

From an early time in our shared career, Christian Sanchez used a mix of filthy language and terms of endearment when referring to the dead at the various crime scenes we shared. One murdered boy was a "cute little fucker," another drowned baby was a "little bug, sleeping away in her own shit," and my favorite, "cocksucker." That one was both a slander and a term of endearment.

After hanging up with the chief, I put away the last supplies and tools for the goat shed, then washed the splattered paint from my hands at the sink next to the chicken coop. It shared a wall with the living quarters, and during renovation, I added a valve so I could turn off the water in the deepest chill of winter, preventing frozen or burst pipes. During the initial tear-out and renovation, I put a lot of effort into ensuring everything was as well-insulated as possible. The barn was way too large to heat, so this was a much easier option. I could make sure I had water out here in winter when I needed it, but I could shut it off when it got too cold.

What now? I wondered. It was late afternoon, and too early to call it a day. Deep down, I knew "what now," but I hid it from myself and disguised it behind the idea to clean and tidy the place some more. *Where there's two, there's more.*

I had made incredible progress in this place in the eighteen months I'd been here, but there was still so much to do, even inside the barn. I'd barely touched the northeast corner, which held the tack room. The two horse stalls inside showed no signs of ever having housed an animal, so I never understood the need for a tack room full of gear. The attached room was not really a room at all, but a raised 12'x20' platform about ten inches above the rest of the floor. It had a four-foot cripple wall along the two sides that shared open air inside the barn, and rows of hooks along the northern and eastern walls, many of them filled with gear that appeared never to have seen a moment of use. Perhaps in the excitement of planning and building this place, the original owner got everything ready for a life as a horseman, but never followed through.

The leaders, bits, and horse gear had a thick layer of dust on them when I first moved in, but in a cursory attempt to tidy up, I had taken his gas-powered leaf blower and directed it at the gear wall, countertop, and stools to get the bulk of the dust out of the area. When I did this, I had a powerful floor fan nearby to sweep the dust out through the large east-side doors. The prairie wind took care of the rest.

I stepped onto the platform and eyed the boxes stacked along the northern wall, beneath the gear hung there. The last time I opened boxes in this barn, just hours ago, I had the first solid PTSD trigger event since moving here, and I wasn't looking forward to another. My brain was firmly telling me not to open any more boxes. PTSD was funny that way in that no matter how innocent or innocuous the action, if there was a trigger attached to it, the brain chemistry took over and pumped up the anxiety volume to eleven. I sensed the rising anxiety but knew better than to fear the mysterious unknowns within an old banker's box. I should focus on cleaning and tidying the barn.

"It's a fucking box!" I said out loud as I stood before the one I had pulled off the stack of twelve. Without hesitation, I pulled the fitted lid off, and I knew right away that my brain was being stupid for causing this kind of anxiety. It was full of old leather straps and bits, as if the previous owner had stocked up on used gear before deciding to buy new stuff. Another box held more of the same. With ten boxes remaining, I felt pretty good about telling my brain to shut up about fear and anxiety. I dove into the third box and found nothing but paper: readouts from some kind of report, along with triplicate forms with the data boxes filled in by hand.

I set it aside and looked at the fourth box as if it were a coiled snake poised to strike. "It's just a fucking box!" I said again, in case I hadn't heard myself the first time. This one was no different from the others, except it may have had less dust. Someone had made some scribblings on the side, but those were the only differences. I grabbed the handle, pulled it from the wall a couple of feet, and yanked the lid off.

Nothing new. More gear. On top were a few more leather straps, varying in length and width. They differed from the others, but I took a handful out and placed them aside. Underneath them, the interesting material began. Underneath them, I found the handcuffs. Several pairs. And leg cuffs. And belly chains. And zip cuffs. And a ball gag. *Of course, there would be a ball gag*, I thought.

The sensation that swept over me differed from the earlier one. There was no panic attack, no troubled breathing, no flash of heat. Just coldness. The kind of coldness I used to share with Laura. The sort of coldness that kept my brain safe from the horror of the realization that came to me. *Where there's two, there's more.*

With two dead bodies in the field, a box of souvenirs, and now a second box of what appeared to be toys for either an adult play party or a torture session, it became clear what we had here. We had someone who enjoyed himself too much to stop at merely two bodies. There would be more out in that field. If that old fucker weren't already dead, I'd have wanted to kill him. Someone needed to be killed for this. Not in a white rage. Not in a fireball of violence; merely an elimination.

I knew what I had to do. Call the chief? No. I had to go drink heavily and drink quickly before my brain exploded. My years of self-reflection and post-incident counseling had taught me that alcohol was one of the weakest tools to use when a trigger struck, but I told myself that this wasn't a trigger. I had recognized it and shut it down before it would become one, so the alcohol wouldn't be a weak tool in this case. That seemed to make sense at that moment.

It was a couple of hours before the girls usually went to bed, but to lure them into their enclosure early, I grabbed the red can and scooped up a bunch of the bean-and-seed mixture I'd bought in bulk from one of my new buddies at the silo for cheap. The girls knew the sound of plastic on seed and came running immediately. I scattered the feed mix in the coop and the neighboring enclosure, then made sure all the kids were home for the night before I secured the outer door. Usually, I'd shut the door between the coop and the small inside pen to deny the hens an errant place to roost, but since they'd be up for a while longer, I'd let them play. I didn't plan on being sober enough in two hours to remember to shut it at their proper bedtime.

Once inside, I walked to the cabinet above the refrigerator and reached for the bottle of Blanton's bourbon that had sat there, unmolested, for several months. Tonight, the horse atop the bottle was lifted off, and the short-term solution to my problem would flow freely. Whoever might be out in the field could wait another day.

11

4 years earlier

She was dead, and there wasn't a goddamn thing that Warren or anyone could do about it. She was more dead than anything he'd ever seen because of the enormity of the life and potential ahead of her that had been snuffed out. Ended by her own choice. Ended because the idea of living another moment in this world was more painful than the few minutes it would take to make it all go away.

Warren stood passively and took it all in: the contents of the closet, the white terry-cloth belt from an absent bathrobe, and the naked eleven-year-old girl hanging at the end of it.

The call about a possible suicide came a few minutes after midnight and directed Warren to go to a lovely and safe part of town south of the Country Club Plaza. Though assigned to East Patrol, he was the closest available unit, so dispatch sent him to Metro to catch this one. Down past the rustic stone buildings of the city's finest shopping and dining neighborhood and across Brush Creek, the homes were large, and the well-kept residential areas were highly sought after by the town's well-to-do.

Not everyone wanted to live out in the suburbs of Lee's Summit or Overland Park. Those with roots in this town, or those who sought to be seen and noticed by the city's powerful, needed a place centrally located to the action. If you were like Raymond Silva, you wanted to be close to monitor your many businesses, legal or otherwise. You wanted an opulent-but-not-too-opulent home to entertain and impress the other players, a castle in which to play King.

The king wasn't home when Warren arrived. He stopped his patrol vehicle in front of the next house south, left the flashers on, and radioed in his status and location. He had silenced the sirens two blocks away; a Metro unit called out on the radio that she was twelve minutes out. He wanted to wait, but a middle-aged Hispanic woman, presumably a housekeeper, had seen him, had come out of the building in near panic, and had begged him to go inside now!

In a mix of English and Spanish, she explained the girl was dead, that she was dead. She was dead! She said she knew the girl was in trouble, but never expected this. Warren's Spanish was good, but the housekeeper spoke so rapidly that he couldn't quite keep up.

"*He* has something to do with this!" she said, so as to spit filth out of her mouth.

She had grabbed him outside the front door and pulled him upstairs past the sitting room and down a short hallway to the girl's room, to what should have been her sanctum. If Warren had tried to imagine what the bedroom of a well-to-do, eleven-year-old stepdaughter of a Made Man would look like, this was it. The room was for Silva's little princess. Twelve-foot ceilings, a four-poster bed, enough white and pink lace to smother an entire herd of My Little Ponies. The housekeeper led him to the door, but he stayed outside in the hallway.

"She's in the closet," she whispered as if not to disturb the girl's sleep.

Warren crossed the room's threshold and stepped gingerly on an obvious path to the closet. As he walked, he observed the toys and trinkets on the bed, on the dresser, and aligned in a corner. There were posters on the wall for K-Pop bands he had never heard of, but the mix of childish things, tech toys, and posters of young heartthrobs told him the girl was preparing to step into the next phase of her life. She was still a child, but she was beginning to recognize a world beyond toys and dolls.

None of that exploration and evolution mattered because Cassandra was dead.

To do what she needed to do in the closet, she had taken the bulk of the clothes off the rack and placed them neatly on her bed. She'd arranged the shoes on the floor and stacked them one on top of another. Pushed back against the closet wall was a small, pink step stool. Before today, it had been used to grab toys from the tops of dressers or from low shelves. Tonight, it was used as a point from which to step into a final abyss.

Cassandra's body was hanging dead center of the rod and square in the middle of the doorway. Nowhere to hide, but she didn't want to hide anymore. She wanted everyone to see her. She appeared freshly showered, her hair beautifully brushed, as if she had primped and preened for a meet-and-greet with a music idol. Naked—no jewelry, just a touch of blush, mascara, and lipstick. Cassandra wanted to be pretty one last time.

Warren felt something shut off inside of him. Not so much of a click but more like a light that's been switched off but whose glow takes a few seconds to fade fully. It took him months to figure out what had shut down, but he eventually discovered it was the part of him that wanted to feel any love or compassion for humans ever again. The part of his brain or heart that wanted to care for and nurture other humans died that night.

He stood as still and quiet as he could, taking in the gruesome scene. Cassandra was a beautiful, beautiful girl, but she was utterly lifeless. A coolness came from her. She was on the cusp of adolescence, her slim, athletic body beginning to swell into womanhood, but so very clearly a girl. A dead girl. A beautiful dead girl.

Procedure stated that when signs of death are so obvious, the body shall be kept as is to keep the scene intact. Don't approach, don't touch, don't contaminate. Warren disregarded procedure and, with a smooth, practiced motion, loosed the lock blade knife in his right pocket. With his left hand and right palm, he gently spun the girl so he could support her as he cut her down. He placed his left knee below her buttocks and reached his left arm around her and across her child's chest to take her weight. The blade made quick work of the bathrobe's belt, and her full weight fell onto Warren. With another smooth motion, he closed the knife and returned it to its home, and he backed out of the closet and a few feet back into the room.

He laid the girl down as gingerly as he could and stood up. In the stronger light of the room, he could see the bruises. They were faint, but they were there. A few were circling her neck, but he couldn't make sense of them because the marks from the rope were mixed in and were more prominent. The bruises on her hips were more pronounced. There were two circles on the uppermost part of her hips, below her navel, centered and about four inches apart from each other.

What part of Warren that had died a few minutes earlier came roaring back to life only to be crushed again as he realized what had caused these bruises—a man's thumbs. He grabbed the small tactical flashlight that he kept in a side pocket of his protective vest, turned it on its lowest setting, and knelt on his right knee next to Cassandra's left side. Shining the light on the backside of her left hip, Warren broke protocol again and lifted her ever-so-gently where he saw the other bruises, four of them in a near-vertical line near the top of her left buttock.

He lowered her back, leaned back, resting his elbow on his knee, and looked at her again, taking in the mix of beauty and horror. Her eyes opened, and she looked directly at Warren.

"Do something!" she whispered.

12 - Thursday

I opened my eyes a moment after Cassandra's ghost did, her whispered words still echoing. There was no chance of sleep whenever she visited, and I knew not even to try. The thing to do was to get up and work, move. The aspirin helped, but there was still a twinge of pain from the soiled blood vessels in my brain. *Better bourbon than red wine*, I thought.

Rarely was I awake before Big Red, but with a bare sliver of light on the eastern horizon, he'd cry out any minute. Grabbing my phone and flashlight, the same one from my time as a patrolman years before, I stepped outside and did a complete lap around the perimeter of the yard near the house. Before I let the girls out to play, I wanted to make sure there were no bad guys around. The prairie held all manner of animals that would be happy to pick off a stray hen: skunks, raccoons, martens, weasels, owls, and the peak predators here, coyotes. We'd been lucky so far and hadn't lost any of the flock; the laws of nature dictated that it would eventually happen. If you're going to free-range chickens, you're at considerable risk of having a few predated upon.

Not yet, though. I credited my vigilance to these early-morning rounds, as well as to what some might consider a disgusting habit, but I saw it as essential for keeping varmints away. I read in an agricultural magazine once that smaller predators won't come around if they smell a larger animal's urine. That nugget of biological wisdom, mixed with the pure joy of peeing out on the open prairie in the dark, on my land, made me more than happy to use science to ward off a threat to the girls.

Remembering what I had found the evening before interrupted this moment of peace—the find that inspired me to drink past my limit, the box found on the tack room floor. Finishing my task, I reached into my pocket for my phone and called the chief.

"Yeah?" said Sanchez in a sleepy but succinct tone.

"You'd better come out here again. I found something."

"Twenty minutes," the chief responded and signed off. At this point in our friendship, Sanchez knew better than to question me when I made a request like this. I wouldn't have hesitated if she had said to jump.

I stood facing north, at the distant hills and the field between. Two bodies in two days were two bodies more than I wanted ever again. No doubt, more were coming.

Behind me, still in the coop, Big Red let the world know that a new day had begun.

"You're late!" I yelled back at him and headed into the barn to grab some feed for the girls. I spread it into the compost bin as the sliver of light rose in the east.

When the chief arrived, I was waiting on the porch with a mug of coffee ready for her. I had another pot of coffee brewed, as I had already worked through most of the first one. I wanted plenty more to go around as the day was sure to be a long one.

"Good morning, Chief." I smiled a fake smile.

"Howdy, Warren. Been a while," the chief returned as she took the offered mug of coffee. Black, always. "Why the early call today?"

"C'mon. Walk with me. I'll show ya." I walked toward the east side barn entrance with the chief. "So, we found the first one in the field by random chance. The next one became a possibility after I found the box with the trophy from the first girl."

"So, what's your point?" the chief asked. It was still early, and the coffee hadn't worked its charm yet.

I led the chief through the open chicken coop door and into the barn proper through the inner coop door. I went to the outer barn door, grabbed the two-by-four that served as the latch for a heavy-duty slider lock, removed it, and swung both doors wide open. The early morning sun was still low on the horizon and glared into the barn.

"There!" I said, pointing to the last box I had found last night. "Go check it out and tell me if you think the same thing I do."

The chief paused, perhaps because she already knew where this was leading. I held back my opinion, knowing she should make this determination. After examining the box's contents and seeing the collection of Baker's tools, her decision was easy. I could see she had reached the same conclusion I had already come to: that the first box I had found was a collection of trophies and that there were even more girls in the field. *Where there's two, there's more.*

13

Within an hour, two other WPD officers were on-scene, as were two volunteer COPs (Citizens on Patrol) from the county department. The crime scene team was en route, but this time, they were from the state. That team had the proper seismic gear to conduct a thorough search of the subsoil across every inch of Warren's triangle of land.

The chief was awaiting the written consent to search she and Warren had verbally agreed to before tearing things up, but she let her two officers sort through the piles of boxes and gear stacked and strewn around the barn. They agreed the team could search every square inch of land outside, and anything inside the barn was fair game. Warren refused to allow the interior of the living quarters to be searched, saying he had found nothing of value there. Plus, when Warren renovated it, he stripped it down to the studs, and since the chief visited often, she knew without a doubt that there were no hiding places within. *Fair enough*, the chief thought. Yet still, she wanted the form signed and in hand ASAP.

The two officers, Langhorne and Pedersen, reported to the scene in grubby civilian clothes because the boss told them they'd be getting dirty. Fine with them. They were both on overtime, and this work was easy. They were going through the barn, pulling any sealed or closed boxes into the middle of the room, but hadn't begun opening any yet. That would wait until the chief said so. Until then, they worked on creating an impressive pile.

Larry Fuller pulled up in his white cargo van. A clear label on the side of it marked that the team was from the Idaho State Police crime scene unit. Fuller and two assistants came out and headed right to the chief.

"'Mornin', Chief!" he said straightaway. "We have a consent form signed yet?"

Before he could answer, the chief got a call on her cell phone. "Yeah?" she barked.

It was Tamala Markus, the city attorney. "Check your tablet. I sent it over." She hung up without waiting for an answer.

"Warren!" the chief yelled, and when she saw his acknowledgment, she pointed to her Ford Explorer. She headed there herself, opened the passenger door, and pulled a tablet from her duty bag. After thirty seconds of waiting for a connection, she checked her email and saw a new one from Markus. She opened it, saw it held a PDF of the consent form, and clicked the appropriate link. It opened up in the Acrobat app, and she reviewed it one last time before handing it to Warren for his signature.

"Look good to you?" she said while he skimmed it.

"Yeah. It's what we said."

"Good! Touch the pen icon and sign in the box with your finger," the chief commanded gently, and Warren complied. He handed the tablet back to his friend. The chief reviewed it again, hit submit, added the new document to a reply email to Markus, and CC'd herself and Warren.

The chief looked at Fuller and his team and said one word: "Go!"

She strode over to her officers and gave them the go-ahead to open the boxes. Each one, whether it held something nefarious, would be cataloged. Each box was to be numbered, and its location mapped. If it had nothing of note, the contents would be listed and go in the benign pile. If it held evil or something dark, it would be noted, the box securely resealed, and returned to the state lab in Pocatello for a thorough examination. When they were done with that, the two would go over all the loose items strewn or stacked in the barn to look for anything obvious: weapons, evidence of a body, or anything out of the ordinary, all of which might take a couple of days.

Despite the gravity and gruesomeness of the situation, Fuller and his team seemed excited about this search. They knew it would be tedious, but they were pleased to use their new toy, a Silas-Clegg hammer, for the first time. The technology was simple: hit the dirt with a large pneumatic hammer at a preset PSI and read the waves it emitted. Within the first few hits, the sensor can gauge how quickly concussive waves travel in this soil and detect anomalies.

Fuller tried to explain some of its intricacies to Sanchez, but she wasn't in the mood.

"Larry, I'm sure it's fascinating, but can we go over the details another time? My brain's elsewhere right now."

Deflated, Fuller went back to his team. They grabbed the heavy storage cases from the back of the van and headed for the far southwest corner of the property.

Sanchez's next order of business was to talk to the volunteer COPs again and give them additional instructions: stay in place, don't allow any non-department people into the area, and radio out if any authorized units arrived.

"Lastly," she made sure to emphasize this part, "take note of anyone paying more attention to the area than they should be. The press may come, but that's expected. I'll deal with them. Just keep 'em back. What I really want to know is if someone not a cop or a reporter is paying too much attention to all this. Make a note of them and their vehicles. Call it in to dispatch, too."

14

The last thing Sanchez needed to do was kick me out of my home for a couple of days.

This farmland was beginning to feel like home, like a safe space, and I hadn't had that for years. Maybe it was good with Laura for a while, but that wasn't really my space. It was our space, even though it didn't last long. With this place at risk of being spoiled, perhaps impermanence is more normal for me than not. Who are those strange folks who can stay peacefully in one home for long periods of time? For decades. How does one attain that level of comfort?

"Yeah, I expected that," I said on the front porch when the chief gave me the news. "You don't need me hovering around, and I sure as hell don't want to see you tearing my dirt up. I already have some things packed."

"Where you gonna stay?" the chief asked. "There's only one hotel in town. Quite a few along the highway in Post Falls, too."

"Nah!" I said with a shrug. "The Rathdrum will do. It has a bar, right? I feel like drinking too much, and this'll give me a chance to meet the locals. That'll be fun."

"Probably not, but okay," Sanchez said. "That'll work. You'll be close to your place, and you can have an officer escort you in if you need to get anything."

"I'll need to take care of the birds and collect their eggs," I said with more affection than Sanchez had heard from me in a while.

"Cool. I'll put them in tonight and put word out to my guys and Fuller's team that they're to let them in and out as needed. No reason to let the kids suffer when Mommy and Daddy are away." The chief knew I loved my birds and that they were a healthy part of my life now. She wanted me to understand that the girls would be okay with all this mess.

"Now grab your shit and get out of the way. Leave the coffee pot." The chief turned and walked away. That was more emotion than she seemed comfortable with. I was alone on the porch, an Ameraucana hen keeping me company. She eyed me for a bit before returning to peck at the gravel.

"Who's a good chick chick?" No one else was around to see or hear me talking to one of the girls like this.

I'd miss them for the brief time I'd be away, but I turned and walked back into the home. After packing a few things into a go-bag in the bedroom, I went into the closet. I kneeled and pulled away a part of the carpet and padding from the far wall. Under that was the concrete foundation, but I had chiseled out a cove for a medium-sized floor safe during the renovations. On top of that was a wooden hatch that lifted easily. The safe had a keypad combination lock and a palm reader, and I needed to use both to open the unit. From the inside, it was firmly bolted to the surrounding concrete, so it wasn't going anywhere without the house being demolished.

Opening it, I reached in, grabbed one of the already opened packs of 100s, removed the rubber band, peeled off $2000, replaced the band, and put the pack of bills back into the safe. With the cash in my pocket, I grabbed my bag and headed to my Honda. Time for some reckless drinking.

15

The Rathdrum Inn was the heart of Westwood's downtown, a hundred feet east of the police station and directly across Main Street from the tetanus-friendly daycare center. Before electricity or automobiles, Westwood was the seat of Kootenai County, and the streets and old buildings still bear witness to that former prestige. Though most of the once-proud downtown had disappeared, a few relics from the old days held fast and carried into the new millennium. The inn was one such place.

Initially built in 1887, The Rathdrum Inn had lived several lives: mercantile, bank, warehouse, bordello, flophouse, and, since after World War II, a bar and hotel. Two major fires had ravaged downtown Westwood over the years, but The Rathdrum survived. New plumbing and other upgrades here and there, along with new neon bar signs, were added, and the video games were swapped out every few years, but other than these cosmetic changes, The Rathdrum Inn was a throwback.

There was a mountain behind the bar. His name was Murphy Longman. If one were to get a silverback gorilla to wear a white dress shirt and a white apron, the result would look much like Longman. Despite his leaning forward onto the bar top, the man's size was obvious. I sized him up and guessed him to be 6'5" and at least 325 pounds, with more muscle than fat. The years had been kind to the barman, but there still had been plenty of them. Sixty-ish by the looks of him, clean-shaven and with a lively visage that brightened quickly when I, a new face to the bar, came in.

"Howdy, Boss!" the silverback said from behind the bar. "What's the word?"

"I'll take a room if you have one," I said as my eyes adjusted to the darkness inside. I looked around to spy the place, but we were alone.

"We have plenty of rooms this time of year. Not a whole lot of reason to visit this early in the spring. Once the hunting seasons open up, it'll be a different story. We just finished up the time when the log haulers hole up for a few nights, so we have plenty of space available. The kitchen opens up in a few minutes, too. Got corned beef today. Made it myself." Longman said with evident pride.

I couldn't see where the kitchen might be, but I noted the smell of brown sugar, vinegar, salt, and beef. It wasn't until then that I realized that I'd had nothing but coffee so far this morning. Last night's dinner came in bourbon form, and I noticed my stomach made a few craving leaps and circles at the thought of food.

"You're on the old Baker place, yeah?" Longman said. "You got the Staties out there digging up more bodies? Guess they didn't find them all yesterday, huh?" Murphy Longman did not seem to be a circumspect conversationalist.

My response was a raised eyebrow.

"Small town," Longman noted the gesture and let me know what he already knew: Westwood has a gossip network that could rival any town. "We all kinda knew that Cha was a loon, but we didn't quite expect that mess."

My unspoken response was, "Well, if you knew he was a fucker, why the fuck didn't anyone do something about it?" Instead, I asked, "How much for the room?"

Longman had me fill out a quick form and took my cash. He handed me the key to a room on the second floor, in the back corner, and told me a few details about the place. With a word of thanks, I grabbed the key and headed to my new, temporary roost. For the price, the room was as fancy as I expected. Since the mid-'70s remodel, little had been done to update the decor. Faux-wood paneling, bad art on the wall, an old phone on the wood-laminate nightstand, and the brown, industrial carpet brought back memories of my grandmother's house.

I tossed my bag on the dresser, kicked off my shoes, and lay on the orange-and-teal bedspread. While on my back, I placed my palms on my belly and straightened my feet and legs into the most comfortable position possible. I knew it was time to breathe and clear my mind of the accumulated clutter from the recent days.

My meditation style was utterly simple: count the breaths as they rise and fall, moving my focus from one part of my body to the next, scanning for tension or unease. I'd always start at the feet and slowly move upwards to the top of the head. Never in my experience have I kept my mind clear for the entire session. In fact, I could rarely do it for more than two or three breaths. Stray thoughts would enter and take my focus off my breath, but I could almost always get back on track.

Almost. After all, the goal wasn't to have a clear mind. The goal was to recognize when the intention was off track and to reset focus.

It went well—for about five breaths. Then, the enormity of the past days' events came roaring into play. I had moved up here to carve out a hunk of paradise in the world, but instead, I managed to find a new flavor of horror. The days of being a supercop were over. The days of protecting and serving were memories from a past life. I thought, *Where in this world can I go where I won't trip over death if not Westwood, fucking Idaho?*

My mind had wandered away from the breath count, and I was sure it wasn't coming back. While lying on the bed with my eyes closed, I could feel the tension rising in my spine and into my shoulders and neck. Though faint and probably a self-creation, I could still catch the scent of death and decay in the air. If I stayed still and quiet much longer, I knew what would happen; the ghosts would come in to fill the void. The ghosts of the dead from the crime scenes, the dead girls on my land, the ghosts of lives ripped away by hate and fury, and the ghosts of friends killed in service or by their own hand. It was time to get up.

I moved quickly out of bed, grabbed my shoes, put them back on, stuffed the key and cash into a pocket, and headed to the bar. Though only one flight of stairs and about thirty-five feet, the walk was long and filled with shame and guilt. I knew better. Alcohol never made the ghosts go away. The voices or smell of death wouldn't fade with beer or booze. This current world was fucked, and no amount of narcotics or depressants was gonna make the slightest difference. I knew better, but I went anyway.

Longman was surprised to see me back so soon. "You smell the good grub?" he asked cheerfully.

I threw a big grin back at the old barman and said, "Sure did. Corned beef sounds great. I'll take a Jack and Coke, too, if you don't mind."

16

Once the team from the lab started their digging and measurements, Chief Sanchez didn't need to stick around. Her guys were busy in the barn, and the volunteers kept away anyone who wasn't supposed to be there, so she headed back to the station to take care of a few things. When she sat back at her desk, the budget reports and personnel issues didn't seem to matter nearly as much as a growing pile of dead girls. She tabled those things for a while longer and made a few calls.

Her first was to liaise with the State Police, specifically Captain Greg Petrelli. She gave him an update on his team's work and its progress. It wasn't much, but she wanted to make sure he knew the costly team and their equipment were on the ground and in use. She also asked who in State could provide her with the most accurate list of missing persons in the Inland Northwest for the past twenty years.

As she asked for it, she looked at the list of local missing persons Olivera had compiled. It wasn't nearly as complete as what Petrelli could pull together, but it was a good place to start. The list showed a few details about each missing person: basic bio, residence, workplace, last known description, and location. All of them had been missing before her tenure as chief, so none of the names were familiar, but one bit of data stuck out. One of the missing girls seemed to have worked at the same place that Baker did.

"I can get that put together," Petrelli told her, interrupting her thoughts. "We keep a pretty accurate list at all times. I'll just narrow it down for your needs and send it your way later today. Look, I'll try to keep the Feds out of this as long as I can, but as soon as we identify a body that's from out of state, they'll want to step in. I already got a call from the ASAC in Spokane about this."

"It is what it is, Cap." Sanchez seemed resigned to the fact that she'll have to keep the FBI updated on this case soon. "We may end up needing their help anyway. I'm sure they'll want everything possible on Baker."

That call ended politely, with a promise of good intel coming her way soon. She knew she'd have no chance if a shoving match happened between Westwood PD and the FBI. Better to get her evidence and facts together for a smooth handover. In the meantime, damn if she wasn't gonna do everything possible to identify some of these girls, to bring some rest and closure to these families.

Her next call was to the city attorney. The chief told Markus to watch out for the warrant request she'd send within the hour. It was for Baker's employment records from his former employer, Upriver Mill. Markus said she'd be on top of it and would transmit it to the judge for signature as soon as she received and approved it. Next, the chief called Kootenai County Undersheriff Andre Willits to let him know she'd be working in the unincorporated parts of the county. She didn't legally need county consent to serve a warrant outside of her city, but it would go much more smoothly if you at least let them know when and why you're sniffing around in their world. They usually do the same anytime their deputies step into Westwood for business.

The warrant application was relatively simple to write. Even easier than usual because she had a template ready for such an occasion. There was nothing privileged in the employee records, especially since the subject had passed away. She wasn't sure how many years a business must keep personnel files after termination. She would have to do some research or call Markus later about that.

After her third spell check of the warrant request and confirming it was solid, she affixed her e-signature and sent it to Markus. The green dot next to Markus' name on the screen meant she was online at that moment. In the next moment, the messenger's status bar showed she had read and received the document.

Time for coffee. The two cups from earlier in the morning had come and gone, so it was time to refill and refuel. At this time of day, the coffee flowed heavily, and there was always a cuppa available. Today was no exception. Black coffee was her poison. *Warren can have all that sugary shit,* she thought to herself as she filled up one of the many mugs she had swiped from him and laughed.

She liked that man a lot, loved him, in fact. He was a great cop and a fantastic guy, but there was something inside of him that couldn't continue to handle all the dread and misery that humans impose upon one another. She saw his relationship wither away, and toward the tail end of her time with KCPD, she noticed he was building a reputation for being unhinged and, frankly, kind of an asshole on the street. She kept tabs on the department after she left and was shocked but pleased to hear that he had pulled the plug. Even more so when he called to ask for her help setting up a place in Idaho, she was the one who told him the Baker place was available.

"Fuck!" she said aloud to no one.

Shortly after she sat back down at her desk, the phone rang. It was the city attorney with good news. "I called Judge Connerman's office and got hold of her right away," Markus started. "I had already sent the request, and she was able to review it while I talked her through the case. She said she'd sign it and get it back to us ASAP."

"Hell! That was easy!" the chief said into the phone.

"Easiest one in a while." Markus finished the chat by saying she'd send it along as soon as she got it herself.

The next call was to Langhorne back at Warren's place for an update. "This place is fucked, Chief!" Langhorne said. "Fuller's team has already found two more bodies, and we have a lot of weird shit from the barn. A bunch of stuff that looks like souvenirs, ladies' stuff. Fuller called out the county's meat wagon, but he said he was worried that they'd find more than that van could hold. He's got the state cooler van headed up from Plummer already."

"Fuck!" she said aloud again. This time to everyone. "Just tag and bag what you see. Take shit tons of pics. Get me those pics and a list as soon as you're done. Bring it all here, and we'll sort through it later.

I'm headed out soon, but I'll swing by there on my way back to town."

Her computer screen showed a small waving flag in the corner. New email. She clicked it open while still on the phone and saw that it was the warrant. "Gotta go," she said. She clicked PRINT, and the big printer in her office started warming up. She'd have to call the mayor to tell him about the new bodies, but she'd do that while on the road to the mill.

17

The Upriver Paper Mill had once been a thriving operation. Once, but no longer. There was a time up through the early 1980s when the lack of Canadian competition and federal regulation made North Idaho a gold mine for timber. Upriver was a titan, with its tendrils in felling, transporting, milling, and selling all things timber. Those days had long passed.

The mill sat on unincorporated county land on the outskirts of Athol. On a bad day, the distinct scent of the mill would waft over the popular amusement park along I-95. The park owners knew what they were getting into when they opened the place in 1988, but they honestly hadn't expected the mill to still be in operation after all their struggles.

The mill's most significant handicap was a near-fatal one: limited access to water. In the mid-1980s, the nearby city of Coeur d'Alene and the flat parts of Kootenai County anticipated a real estate boom and needed space for development. As a result, one of the mill's two main tributaries, the larger one, would be diverted and turned into an artificial pond. The mill would still have water from the smaller creeks and grandfathered access to a spring that helped maintain flow. Additionally, operations could ramp up in spring and early summer, when seasonal runoff would increase downstream flow. The EPA had set standards for the mill's water use and waste outflow based on month-to-month river flow.

The early and mid-90s were hell for the mill. Amid significant shifts in production and resources, constant EPA inspections and enforcement, and the grand sum spent on legal challenges and defense, the Mallard family seriously considered shuttering the place and calling it a day. Instead, long past his prime but still considered a lumber baron, Harold Mallard finally retired in '97 and handed the reins to his only child, Gerald.

This was also the time when a steady stream of Californians was heading up here after the first of many real estate booms, bringing up all manner of retired firefighters, law enforcement officers, blue-collar contractors, and their families, all of them flush with cash from the sale of their tiny California homes and looking for a ten-acre parcel in Kootenai County, Idaho. Those parcels would need water, guaranteed by the county and provided by the natural aquifer beneath the prairie and by the many rivers in the area. That meant less for the mill.

Gerald Mallard had grown up around mills his whole life and was no stranger to the operation. He knew someday he'd take over for his father, and he had a plan in place. Despite strenuous objections from the now-retired elder Mallard, the new boss ceased operations except for the main mill and sold off all the other properties and feeder businesses. The plan was to trim the fat, pay off creditors, and stay afloat long enough for fortunes to turn. He'd done all he could under the circumstances, but the fortunes hadn't fully yet turned. Some things improved, but what saved the mill was the alternative income stream the younger Mallard created.

18

Williamson was waiting for the chief when she turned off the gravel strip that led from Brunner Road to the mill's parking lot. A truck with a trailer full of jack pines had pulled onto the road a minute before the chief, and she had followed its dust trail the whole way. As she parked in the lot, the truck continued into the mill's yard and parked near the loading arm.

Williamson's cruiser, an older Ford Explorer, sat parked along a fence next to what had been a security shack. Now, the wooden box served no purpose other than as a demarcation point between the parking lot and the lumberyard. He nodded to the chief as she grabbed her radio and called Central to let them know the two of them were out at the mill. Sanchez was a stickler in this aspect of law enforcement. The baddest bad guy, the fastest car, or the biggest gun can't outrun or outpace a radio. It was one of her ongoing missions to make sure her people remembered that, and to call in every detail possible. Williamson hadn't yet taken on that habit.

"Thanks for coming out. You know any of the guys working here?" she asked. This was her first time visiting the mill, and she hadn't yet had a reason to meet any of its workers.

"Yeah," he said coyly. "A few of them have had families up here forever. I've arrested a bunch of Upriver guys over the years, but I don't know how many of them still work here."

"That's more than I know. Come on. Let's say hello," she finished and headed toward the bigger shack with the "Office" sign above the door.

Gail Mueller sat at her desk and looked surprised by the arrival of two police officers, though she quickly recovered her composure. The desk was an old metal one, the same kind seen in offices around the country since the 1940s. It held an incredible assortment of papers: invoices, manifests, vehicle repair receipts, and a dozen other items the chief couldn't recognize. Along the wall behind her were seven file cabinets of the same color and finish as the desk. Banker's boxes and dozens of storage tubes holding maps or blueprints sat atop each cabinet.

Gail was a heap of a person, not merely in size, but in how she sat at her desk. She was unmoving and seemed to have been in the same position for all of the thirty-seven years she had worked here. The air was thick with the smoke of the cigarette that was perched on her lips. The ashtray was full of the day's butts, and the carcass of an empty pack of Virginia Slims sat at its side. *You've come a long way, baby.*

"Can I help you, officers?" Gail croaked to the chief.

"Yes, ma'am," Sanchez said. "We have a warrant signed by a Kootenai County judge allowing us access to all of the employee records for one of your former employees."

Gail's tension level went up. The chief and Williamson could see it by the stiffening of her posture. Probably upset that someone—a cop, a judge, or anyone—would dare to mess with her precious and meticulously maintained records.

"Yeah?" she asked. "Which employee, dear?"

"Charles Baker."

Gail's face showed nothing new, but given that she had appeared to be a boiling pot slowly gaining momentum only moments earlier, the lack of response to Baker's name was noticeable. She picked up her phone without looking at it and hit two buttons.

"There are a couple of police officers here with a warrant for some employee records," Gail said into the phone. After a pause, she said, "Charles Baker." Another pause, then, "Okay. I'll tell them." For the entirety of the conversation, she never took her eyes off the chief.

"Our operations manager will be down in a few moments," she said calmly and politely. With the call completed, her face softened, as if she had dodged something disquieting. The name of Charles Baker carried a stench that was worse than the years of tobacco ingrained in the paneling. Gail stopped making eye contact and wouldn't do so again for the rest of the visit.

Barry Gillum's appearance was ninety seconds in the making. His office seemed to be directly overhead. His chair squeaked as he apparently rose. His footsteps were loud and heavy as he made his way to his office door. His door opened but did not close, and the noise faded as Gillum headed down the hallway toward the stairs. There was nothing until the sounds picked up again as Gillum descended the second set of stairs. There was no carpeting in the hallway, so each step was more pronounced than the previous one as he approached the doorway to the reception area. Behind her, Williamson took a deep breath, as if bracing for a tense conflict.

"Hello, Officers. What brings you out?" Gillum said, as politely as a used-car dealer.

"I'm Chief Sanchez out of Westwood, and this is Sergeant Williamson. Who are you?" the chief said politely but with authority.

"I'm sorry. I'm Barry Gillum, Operations Manager around here." He continued nervously, "What can I do for you today? Is everything okay?"

"We have a warrant signed by a county judge," Sanchez handed the warrant over as she spoke, "allowing us to access your personnel records for any and all information regarding a former employee of yours, Baker."

Gillum took the warrant and appeared to be reading it, but Sanchez could see his wheels turning. She wondered if he already knew about the discoveries at Baker's home.

"Well, ma'am…" he drawled, "Mr. Baker hasn't worked with us for many years, so I'm not sure what we might still have around here. He passed away shortly after his retirement."

"We'll take whatever you have. I'm sure it will be helpful for what we're doing. I'm certain that you've heard about some goings-on at his property, and I know you'd want to help however you can." After a moment, thinking of the list from earlier, she continued, "I understand that another former mill employee went missing a few years ago. Tracy Goodson. What can you tell me about her?"

Gail gasped audibly at the mention of Tracy, but still kept her eyes away from the chief. "Yeah, Tracy …" Gillum hesitated. "I think I remember her. She was an admin gal while I was still a loader and floor guy. I didn't know her, um, very well." He looked up at Williamson during the last part. "Gail," he turned his attention to the office manager," see what you can find in the files about Charles. She jumped up, as much as her body would allow, happy to have a break from the tension, and headed to the last two file cabinets on the far right.

While Gail flipped through the folders and drawers, Gillum returned to the chief. "Is it … uh, is Tracy one of the girls you've found already?"

"We don't know yet," the chief responded. "It's way too early for that. For now, we're trying to find out more about Mr. Baker. We don't even have enough to say whether he did anything wrong."

It was a lie, of course. She and Warren seemed to be the only two in the town who didn't know Baker was a bastard. Maybe most didn't know the full details about his habits, but it's becoming clear that he was a dirty old fucker, and everyone else gave him a lot of rope.

"Barry," Gail said sheepishly from the corner file cabinet, "there don't seem to be any files at all for Cha!"

19

The chief drove away, wondering if she had overplayed her hand or acted too tough. After Gillum professed ignorance about the missing records, the chief politely yet firmly told him that he and the mill would find them and send them her way ASAP. She handed him her card and directed him to email everything they had to her at the earliest opportunity. If not, she'd be out in a day or so for a less pleasant visit.

She knew what might have happened and didn't expect ever to see any files on Baker. The mill wanted to distance itself from the guy and probably purged everything they had on him. Hopefully, by coming on strong at the next visit, she may shake loose something interesting.

She thought about Tracy Goodson and tried to remember a few details about the girl. All she could recall was that she lived in Athol. On the laptop screen mounted in her vehicle, Sanchez pulled up the girl's record. She brought up any information she could about Tracy and saw that her mother still lived in town, at the same address.

The Crossroads Trailer Park was no better or worse than the dozen or so others that dotted the area. That meant it was as dirty and run-down as the rest, long past its glory days. Also, it had no glory days. It was home to only a few permanent residents. That could be seen in the extra effort put into those trailers: flowerpots, patio furniture, and a carport. The rest were in various states of decay and dilapidation. These were rented or lent to temporary or seasonal workers who hauled or cut timber in North Idaho—plenty of dead cars and empty beer cans.

Lana Goodson lived in the second trailer on the right from the park's entrance, a then-resplendent 1971 model that was the envy of the neighbors back in the day. Today, the faint pink hue of the aluminum exterior had lost its luster, and the roof seemed a repository for pine needles and cottonwood pollen. The chief parked in a guest space a few yards inside the entrance and walked to Goodson's home. Standing on the front steps, she heard the television on and someone walking after she had knocked.

"Mrs. Goodson?" the chief asked. The woman in the housecoat nodded. "Hello. Sorry for the interruption. I'm chief of police over in Westwood, and I wanted to know if I could ask you a few things about your daughter, Tracy."

The mention of her daughter set her back for a moment. "You're the chief?" she asked, puzzled. "But you're a woman."

"Yes, ma'am. Chief Christian Sanchez," she smiled. "They let girls become police officers now." The line came out as a weak joke, she hoped. Moving to North Idaho had many benefits, yet the region's older residents were not the most forward-thinking. She had encountered this attitude and thought she was used to it. Sometimes, though, it still pissed her off.

With a polite smile, she continued, "May I come inside and ask you about Tracy?"

"Of course," Lana said. "Come in and make yourself comfortable." The initial shock wore off, and her manners returned. "May I get you some coffee or tea? I always have a pot on."

"That would be wonderful, ma'am. Coffee, please. Black." The open floor plan let the chief see and chat with Lana as she entered the kitchen.

"I've gone through all the official records of your daughter and her disappearance," the chief said. "As I'm sure you know, there have been a lot of young girls going missing in the past fifteen years or so. Even though there haven't been any disappearances for a while now, I want to make sure that the girls aren't forgotten. I want to keep them in mind as we go forward. Tracy still matters. Each of those girls still matters, and I want to ensure we remember that.

"Now, I'm very sorry if talking about it causes pain or sadness, but I hope you understand that I don't want this to happen to any more girls or their families."

"Yes. I understand, Chief," Lana said softly as she filled a cup for the chief. Her lack of eye contact was noticeable as she handed over the mug.

Sanchez noticed the avoidance. "Thank you, Lana. Call me Chrissy, please," said the chief.

* * *

No one called her Chrissy anymore. Chrissy was that little girl growing up outside of Sedalia, Missouri. Chrissy was the youngest of three farm kids. Chrissy raised sheep in 4-H.

101

Cute little Chrissy disappeared at seventeen years of age when she had to fight for her life against a drunk trucker who thought that his sweet little waitress at the truck stop cafe had wanted him. He had waited for her when she got off her late shift, getting drunker as the time went by. He knew she was flirting with him when he had dinner and wanted to return the favor and give her the night of her young life. He'd make Chrissy a woman.

Christian was born that night when she fought him off with kicks to the groin and an elbow to the bridge of his nose. Christian found power at the same time that Chrissy died, never viewing the world the same way ever again. Her two older brothers loved her, but they had been merciless in their taunting, teasing, and wrestling with her. Every move the trucker tried on her to get control, her brothers had done before. She knew how to move in defense.

More kicks to the groin. Elbow to his ribs. Forearm to the throat. A bite on his wrist. Knee to the midsection.

The trucker collapsed and slowly moved into a defeated sitting position as Christian stood over him, awaiting the next move. Behind her, footsteps, and she turned briefly to see Miguel, the line cook, slowly walking toward them. She noticed the baseball bat in his hand at roughly the same time that he figured out what had happened. He stood next to her, looked at the beaten man, looked back at Chrissy, paused—and with a swing that would make Stan Musial proud, gave the trucker a goodnight kiss. Christian watched.

No one called her Chrissy anymore.

* * *

"Of course, Chrissy," Lana said, visibly softening and looking directly at the chief. The name did the trick. Sanchez was both proud and ashamed that the cheap gimmick worked.

"I'm not sure what more I can tell you. I really don't recall much from that time," Lana started. "I've read the reports, and I certainly recall what they say and what I told the deputies back then, but I just don't have any memories of my own. I've shut out so much."

The chief listened but turned away to look at the pictures on the hallway wall near the kitchen. "Did you know any of her coworkers at the mill? She had been there for a couple years. Did she hang out with any of them? Date anyone?" So many pictures on the wall, none of them new. "Who is this in this picture with Tracy?"

The picture showed two beautiful humans, full of fun and life, gathered around a campfire. "Oh, that's Aaron. My son. That picture was taken the fall before she disappeared," Lana said blankly.

"Does he live around here?" she asked. Maybe he'd know more about her dating habits and social life.

"No," Lana said firmly. "He's dead, too."

"I'm very sorry," Sanchez mumbled, shocked at the woman's double trauma. "I'm sorry. I don't know what to say."

It was true. She was blank.

A thought struck the chief, and she turned back to the photo at the campfire. Tracy was a beautiful young woman. The camera caught her mid-laugh, at the height of joy with her brother by a bonfire, surrounded by her friends and family on a chilly, crisp autumn night. A cool night, but still no snow or ice, so all she needed for warmth was the fire and a yellow Aeropostale zippered hoodie—a hoodie similar to one the chief had seen just yesterday.

"Lana," the chief asked, "do you have anything of Tracy's still around? Anything I can look through?"

20

In his patrol car on the way back to town, Williamson heard Sanchez call out at an address in Athol. A quick reverse search showed that the resident of that address was Lana Goodson.

Fuck! he thought to himself. *More old business. More of Cha's bullshit from yesterday making a mess today.*

He'd worked to keep the last chief from piecing together Baker's activities, going so far as to *disappear* one man to whom Cha revealed too much.

* * *

Gerald Mallard listened to Gillum's voicemail as soon as the notification popped up on his phone's screen. He had seen when Gillum tried to call, but didn't answer because he was already pissed at Gillum and didn't want that to show in his voice. After listening to the message, he was doubly glad he had waited.

He had already received word about the chief's visit and how it went, so he was already primed to be upset. The fear and nervousness in Gillum's voice in the message told him more than he wanted to know about the kid's state of mind.

He had waited about thirty minutes before calling Gillum back. He played it cool on the phone. "Barry," he started gently and in a calm tone, "first of all, calm the fuck down. We've been through this a bunch of times, and it always works out, doesn't it?"

"Yes, Mr. Mallard, but this is the first time this new chief has been involved." As Gillum spoke the sentence, his words got faster and louder as he went. "Plus, she asked a few questions about Tracy. No one's asked about her in years."

"Well, they're pulling up a few bodies at Cha's place, so you'd expect them to start asking, right?"

Mallard did his best to keep his voice calm and his words comforting. Gillum had proven to be a useful idiot over the years, but an idiot nonetheless. He had to keep him calm.

"Hey, kid. Are you a little extra nervous because it's that time of the month?" the older man said with a smile and a half-chuckle, proud of his pun. It worked.

"Yeah," Gillum said sheepishly on the other end of the call. Mallard could even hear some lightness in the kid's voice.

"That part is gonna go smooth as always. We're all a little nervous at the end-of-month swaps, but nothing is going to interfere with that. Nothing ever does. It had fucking better not. Am I right?" Mallard wanted that to come out lighthearted, but it didn't quite work.

Gillum stayed silent. He continued, "Reardon's guys will come up and get their loads, pay us, and be on their way. Smooth and easy. We don't want to do anything to make anyone nervous now. So far, there's nothing in the news about it, and that should hold another day or so. We just need to get everything loaded tomorrow and be ready for the swap-out the next day."

Still nothing from the other side of the

conversation. Gillum had proven to be a good enough choice as his fixer after Cha retired, but only because the kid was smart enough not to think for himself. He wasn't bright by any definition of the word, but he could follow orders to the letter. Gillum had never liked his wife, but her long-expected departure a few years ago threw him into a tailspin. He'd been getting sloppy lately. Sloppy drunk, too. He was never drunk at work, but he often showed signs of a hangover or smelled like he'd slept in his clothes. The kid had to keep his shit together for another couple of days, and Mallard would deal with it after that.

"Okay, boss," Gillum said. "I'll have Gail email the chief with scans of whatever we may have for Cha, and I'll have her say that we're reaching out to the accountant for more in the archives."

"That'll keep her happy for a couple days. That's all we need for now." Mallard ended the call without saying goodbye. A ping in his ear signaled he had received a text during the call. As he didn't know if or how he could check while still talking, he hurried through the last part of his chat with Gillum.

He found the right buttons to see his texts and what had been sent.

The Chief is at Lana Goodson's house.

More great news, he thought to himself as he reached into his drawer for the bottle of Old Grand-Dad bourbon that he had kept there for such moments.

21

Tracy Goodson's room was in the same condition as when she had first disappeared. Years earlier, Lana had used it as a storage area for a few extra things, but all of Tracy's belongings remained. Her dresser was full of clothing and personal items; the walls still held a few posters and mementos; and the closet was packed with more clothes. Everything looked like it was from a twenty-something's room in 2007. On top of the dresser was a pile of CDs: Fall Out Boy, Avril Lavigne, and Nelly Furtado. The one on top, from Linkin Park, had an autograph on the cover, presumably from a band member. Grabbing it, the chief opened it and saw that the disc was in its place, but the plastic case held two other items: a ticket stub from the band's show at the Spokane Arena that summer and a picture taken at the show. The photo showed the concert stage in the background, but the focus was Tracy's big, beaming smile, wrapped in a loving, excited embrace with her date for the night, Barry Gillum.

"Huh!" Sanchez said out loud.

The chief examined the remaining CD cases and dresser drawers but found nothing noteworthy. There was nothing of interest in the nightstand or beneath the mattress, and the boxes stacked along the wall near the bed appeared to be filled with Lana's household items—not anything belonging to Tracy.

The closet floor was full of shoes: dress shoes, work shoes, and going-out shoes. Sanchez noted she lacked the part of her brain that made women love shoes. Sure, she had a few, but nowhere near as many as this Imelda Marcos-inspired collection. She methodically checked the pockets of every item hanging on the rod from one side of the closet to the other. Nothing worthwhile or interesting. The shelf above the rack held several boxes, some decorative, some merely functional. The decorative boxes held a variety of winter gear: hats, scarves, and the like. Another held intimate wear and swimsuits, and yet another held more mementos, including two journals. Flipping through the scribbled thoughts and quotes that filled the pages, Sanchez saw that Tracy had made the last entry when she was still a teen. High school stuff, mainly. Nothing from her days at the mill or regarding Barry.

Two boxes remained. The first one she brought down was a box that had once held reams of paper. Now it held Tracy's personal and financial documents: tax information, bank account statements, checkbooks, and an assortment of employee paperwork from the mill. Nothing exciting.

The second box was a banker's box, much like she had seen earlier at the mill and in Warren's barn. It was lighter than expected, filled with clipped newspaper articles about the mill and the various EPA investigations from 2005 to 2007, along with two bundles of folders. The articles addressed some of the mill's offenses and the fines levied against it. A few quoted the mill owner, Gerald Mallard, saying how he takes these violations seriously and will do his part to make them right. "Upriver Mill has been a partner in the county for decades, and we want to continue being a good neighbor for years to come."

Sanchez grabbed one of the two packs of manila folders—the thicker one. The rubber band that had held the ample contents together for years broke as she tried to remove it. Inside the folders were several bundles of documents, each held together with a binder clip. Each bundle had a cover page that appeared to be an EPA form completed by a mill employee, and behind it were copies of in-house inspection forms from the mill showing water-sample readings and greenhouse gas discharge data, along with the mill's weekly self-disclosure forms. Other forms in each pack showed the volume of truck traffic entering and exiting the mill lot, as well as the total weight of each load type. Still more papers contained neat reports of exports to out-of-state buyers. Near the back of each bundle was a series of Customs and Border Protection forms, one from each truck from Canada, showing its load, volume, and any tariffs paid when entering the U.S. The packets were in chronological order from January 2005 until July 2007, the month Tracy disappeared.

The second bundle was slightly thinner than the first. It too was arranged by month and covered the same period. The major difference between the two was that many of the forms that were neatly typed in the first bundle had been handwritten in the second. None of the forms or reports in the second bundle had the more extensive numbers and test results that the first ones did. The date ranges were the same, and they both looked like EPA forms, but the data for correlating months differed between the two sets. Double-checking, she noticed that June 2007 was missing from both groups.

Sanchez could discern enough data from the reports to determine that the discrepancies probably meant something, but she didn't know what. Lana said she didn't know what the papers were about either, but she couldn't bear to throw anything out, so she kept them all these years. She'd bring them back to the station and sort it out later. After getting permission to take a few things, she said her goodbyes to Lana.

22

I was feeling great! My sour mood had long since disappeared, and I was sure it was because of my happy belly from the better-than-expected corned beef. It had nothing to do with the six drinks I'd had in the last few hours.

I was a responsible drinker, or so I told myself. For every alcoholic beverage, I'd also drink a glass of water. Plus, I'd save one of the stir sticks from each beverage on the bartop with me to help keep track of how much I had to drink. Since my commute home was only a few feet, I allowed myself to drink more than I usually would at a pub. The thought struck me that this was, in fact, the first time I'd visited a pub in Westwood since my arrival.

During the few hours I'd spent on my barstool throne, a few folks had come in for a late lunch or a quick drink, but other than a quick nod or a polite greeting, no one stayed long enough to strike up a worthwhile chat. Mostly, I surfed on my phone, read the news, did some administrative housekeeping, and got a big dopamine fix from the influx of new electronic information from a world that wasn't Westwood.

Longman dropped another Jack and Coke, and from a tumbler in front of me, the barman grabbed enough cash to cover the drink. I began the binge by placing $100 in it and would let it roll as long as I needed it to. The front door opened.

"Aw, fuck!" Longman said quietly as he saw who stood in the doorway. "It's Trapper Dan!"

Though overcast, the day was still a bright one, and when the new visitor opened the front door of the pub, the wash ruined my vision for an instant. The man stood in the open doorway, and all I could see was his silhouette, 5'10", around 270 pounds, with a wide-brimmed CC Filson bush hat and a matching knee-length duster.

He moved in closer to let the door shut behind him, made a show of removing his aviator sunglasses, and stayed in the doorway for a few extra moments to let his eyes adjust to the darker room. At that moment, I could see that my initial guess about the man's weight was about thirty pounds light.

Trapper Dan moved toward the middle of the bar with a very distinctive gait. Either a few of his lower vertebrae were fused, or he had a back brace that forbade him from having any lateral bend in his lower back. He must have damaged his knees years ago because, as he strode, he barely bent them and instead swung them out to the side more than usual. He used the sway of his ample belly both as a metronome for his pace and as a counterbalance to his knees.

Longman and I watched him as one would watch a float in a parade pass by. Dan made it to a stool in the middle of the bar and sat down.

"Hello, Murph. How's your sister?" he said in a polite voice.

Longman didn't take the bait. "What'll it be, Dan? Bud?"

"That'll do just fine, thanks? Corned beef today?" Dan asked in his most polite voice.

I watched an obviously tense yet overly polite conversation about whether Dan would get the corned beef. He did.

Longman walked away to the kitchen, leaving an awkward silence at the bar. Trapper Dan turned to Warren. "I banged his sister about thirty years ago, and he's never forgiven me."

I was surprised—but not. There had been about thirty seconds of quiet since Longman left, and Dan seemed to be the kind of guy who needed to fill that kind of emptiness with banter. Though I had been paying attention, I had avoided eye contact with the newcomer. I was cradling my glass and watching the ice melt, hoping to avoid a conversation—no such luck.

"So you're a cop, huh?"

"No! Not anymore," I said, continuing to stare at the ice.

Dan continued to probe. "So how many bodies they gonna find at your place?"

There was no escaping it now. It was time to have a conversation with a stranger. To do so required an internal shift akin to an actor putting on a new face. I could do it easily enough. I just didn't want to. The buzz from all the bourbon, sugar, and caffeine had been doing a wonderful job of preventing me from thinking about all the death at home. Alas, no more.

Shifting my gaze from the melting ice to the old trapper, I added a half-smile and said, "Not sure. I want my place back in time to get all the fieldwork done before the rains hit again."

114

Dan raised his bottle. "Well, here's to governmental efficiency and a low body count. That's all any of us can really hope for these days." We lifted our drinks and, in tandem, briefly touched both to the bartop and enjoyed a sip together.

"So, you're a cop?" the old trapper asked the same question again in the same tone that one would ask about the weather. I wasn't sure whether he was being confrontational.

"No. Not for a bit," I replied, but I didn't want to stay on this thread, so I turned it around right away. "You been around here a while? What do you know about Charles Baker?" If I were going to be trapped in a conversation, I might as well get something out of it.

"Me?" Dan started. "I was born up the road in Spirit Lake. Lived there for a spell but took off for a while with the Marines. I blew some shit up for a while and came back. Haven't really left since. Well, that's not totally true. I went to Seattle a couple times to have my heart worked on."

"I gather it went well," I added. "The surgeries, I mean."

"Oh, hell, yeah! I'm right as rain again. I'm good for another fifteen years as long as I keep the batteries on this goddamn thing fresh." Dan pointed to a spot an inch to the left of where his heart would be, presumably for a pacemaker.

"Now, about Baker. Charles was too dignified a name for that fucker! He's been just 'Cha' for as long as I've ever known him. I could tell you a bunch of stories about how shitty he was, but I guess you can figure that out by all the dead girls at your place."

"Yeah," I replied, "that's what we in the business used to call a 'clue.' Tell me about him."

Trapper Dan seemed like a guy who loved to chat and gossip, so not only was this a great way to get a local viewpoint, but it also helped me avoid oversharing. Not that it mattered. It seemed the town knew plenty about me already.

"Imagine a badger but without its usual good manners. Then, add on the drinking habits of ten Irish poets. On top of that, throw in the demeanor of a junkyard dog that hasn't been fed in a while. Get him all good and soused, and the next day, send him to work at the mill, and he'll still be the best man for the job. Everyone will hate him, but he'll get shit done. No one really liked him except the owners of the mills he'd worked for. As long as he produced, they didn't care. Running a mill was a tough gig. Making one profitable was even harder.

"Cha's mom took off early, and his dad was a lumberjack and logger, so Cha followed along. He was a hard worker, but he was always looking for the next step—something with better pay. I worked with him for a few years up at the Doris's mill near Bonners Ferry, but he jumped ship and went to work for Jerry Mallard when he took over Upriver. This must have been around 'ninety-somethin'.'"

Longman came out of the kitchen with a sizeable portion of corned beef, cabbage, carrots, and potatoes. The smell hit me right away, making me hungry again.

"I was just telling our new friend about our old friend, Cha," the trapper said as he cleared a space in front of him for his late lunch. "Thank you, Murph. Looks great!"

"Glad to hear that. Hope you choke on it." Longman grabbed another Budweiser and set it beside the steaming plate of food. "He sure the hell wasn't my friend. I don't think he ever had any. He stopped coming here about twenty years ago, which is fine by me. He was an angry drunk and mostly an asshole when he was sober. You tell him about his last wife and kids, Dan?"

The old trapper took a quick sip of beer before answering. "No. You go right ahead."

"It's a short story, and I'm sure you can figure it out quickly enough," Longman said. "He's got three kids from two of his three wives. He didn't have kids with the last one, thank God. The first two stayed for about five years each before splitting. Escaping, really. The last one, Virginia, lasted a year before she headed out of town. She had been around Westwood forever, but something Cha did made her up and leave. I heard she passed a few years back.

"You'd think someone who is obviously a bastard and whose reputation was shit would have trouble finding one wife, let alone three. I didn't know his first wife, but the second and third, Anna and Virginia, seemed to be attracted to the fear and damage like they could 'fix' him or some shit. Nice gals. Just not terribly bright when it comes to how horrible men can be. After a few years of being beaten up and abused, they finally got learned enough and took off. None of the kids ever came back into town. They didn't even want his land or house. Hope you're enjoying it all, by the way."

"I was." I half-laughed. "Did anyone know about all the bodies?

"No." Dan was back in the conversation. "We all knew Cha was involved with shady stuff at his mill, but I don't think anyone knew about this. The town is talking about him more now than when he was alive. I'm sure the chief is gonna come up with a list of gals that have gone missing in the last twenty years or so. Who knows how many they'll find out there? I only knew a couple of the missing gals, but we mostly assumed they had run off and found new lives. Well…" he paused. "I guess we all kinda hoped that."

They'd said enough. Dan and Murphy, exhausted by the weight of the topic, tried to shift the focus back to me. "So, what's your story?" Longman shifted to this new thread. "How the heck did you manage to make it here? In fact, why here?"

On paper, it was an easy answer, but the recent spate of dead bodies made the whole thing sound silly. "I was tired of being a cop. Tired of dealing with death and liars and child molesters. Tired of administrative bullshit that was more important than stopping folks from hurting each other."

Jack Daniels was loosening my tongue more than usual. "I've found that only a small percentage of people are really shitty, but that small percentage has more of an effect on the rest of the world than the small percentage of saints out there. It's my 10-80-10 rule. You take any group, any demographic: plumbers, schoolteachers, truckers, Libertarians, Senegalese, anything, or any group. Ten percent of those folks are gonna be saints and heroes, living good lives and helping their neighbors when they can. Eighty percent of them are gonna be a mix of folks stumbling around in the world, maybe trying to do good, or maybe just trying to keep their heads down. Folks in this group make good consumers and generally follow most accepted social norms. They may be wise, or they may be idiots, but they're mostly harmless. The last ten percent were guys like Baker. Just rotten and evil, no matter the circumstances."

I paused a moment to gauge the effect my words had on the audience, but instead found that I had pissed myself off with the topic. "I had had enough, and the time to leave popped up, and I was smart enough to go. You probably know that the chief is an old buddy of mine, and she sang praises about this place, so it seemed like a good idea. Now, I'm not so sure."

The silence sat for a moment until Dan asked, "You bang her?"

"God Damnit, Dan!" Longman yelled. "There's no good reason to go asking a question like that. Chief Sanchez has been good for this town, and there's no need to be disrespectful like that."

Trapper Dan held his hands up in full capitulation and walked his words back. "I'm just curious. No disrespect intended to the lady."

"That 'lady'," I smiled, "is one of the baddest motherfuckers you'd ever meet. I never saw her bested in a fight, I never saw her hesitate when things went south, and I never saw her lose her shit when a scene was a madhouse. Solid as a rock, and I'd do anything for her."

Silence.

"But no," I added. "I never banged her. She was always my patrol supe. Nothing sexy about that. In fact, one time, a bunch of us from the unit were drunk at a BBQ, and I was talking crazy shit about being a stud in the sack. I made some stupid crack about teaching her a few things. She looked me dead in the eye and said, 'No thanks, son. I like men.'"

Dan and Murphy smiled at the image.

I continued, "The guys fell out laughing, and I never heard the end of that."

Another silence.

That was enough. Quid pro quo, Clarice.

"Is Upriver still running?" I turned the topic around again. Murphy noticed the empty glass before me and nodded as if to ask if I wanted another. I nodded back in the affirmative.

"Barely!" Dan said. "They do pulp for paper, wood pellets, and by-products. They've been holding on by buying the scraps from the lumber mills and also shitloads from the Canadians. The Canucks get a better price when they sell to us. You'll always see a bunch of their trucks coming south full of shit pines and other low-quality stuff that no other lumber mill could make use of. Mallard chops it all up, loads it full of whatever juice he needs to make it into either pulp for the papermakers or the pellets that he sells in bulk to the distributors."

"What did Baker do there?" I asked.

"Well," Dan began slowly, "his official title was VP of Operations, but what that really meant was that he would get shit done! If something mechanical went wrong, he'd handle it. If there were labor disputes, he'd fire the problem or get someone's ass whooped until they stopped crying. If a Canadian mill or trucking company was screwing around with deliveries or prices, Cha would take care of it. No one really asked questions because shit always got taken care of, and the mill stayed open. Mallard could keep counting his money, and the county could keep another seventeen or so jobs."

"He retired a handful of years ago. Died about six months later in a car crash up in the hills. Old fucker had no business driving those roads." Murphy let the words sit in the air and turned to get another beer for Dan.

After a silence, Dan chimed in, "He thought he was free, that he could escape all the shit he'd done. It just shows you that you can never really escape the past. Karma got him. And you." He looked straight at me. "If you or anyone goes digging through the dirt and dragging the past like you are, you're gonna find more than a bunch of rocks. Sometimes, the past doesn't die."

That was enough socializing for one day. For a month. I had had enough and needed to be in silence for a while. "Hey! Can I grab a 'sixer' of those Buds and bring them upstairs?"

After the lunch, seven drinks, and the six-pack, there was still plenty of change in the tumbler, but I left it all there for the barman. The grub was good, the drinks made me forget for a while, and the information about the players was helpful, but it was time to go cocoon.

23

Williamson was at the station, working on daily reports, when Sanchez returned. She carried the two boxes past him and into her office, giving a "Howdy" along the way. She dropped them on her desk, grabbed an empty coffee mug, and headed to the break room to fuel up. On her way back, Williamson asked her where she had disappeared to after the mill.

"The trip to the mill got me thinking," the chief said, "so I visited Tracy Goodson's mother. She still lives in Athol. Turns out that she hasn't gotten rid of any of her daughter's stuff."

Williamson's heart froze, but his voice remained cool. "Yeah? Find anything good?" *What now? That fucker Warren had already upset my world enough by finding all of the mess that Baker had left behind. That was Gillum's job to clean up at his farm.*

"Yeah," the chief replied. "It was again highlighted to me that I lack the Shoe Gene." Williamson was about to say something, but the chief continued. "The two boxes you saw have some personal records of Tracy's, but also a lot of inspection records from the mill for a period in the mid-aughts up until Goodson disappeared. Lots of EPA inspection stuff that I can't yet make sense of. Also, it seems that Gillum knew Tracy more than he let on." The chief showed Williamson the photo on her phone that she had snapped of the two of them at the concert.

"So," she continued, "we have a missing girl who saved documents from her employers, a mill manager who is denying his relationship with her, and a growing pile of dead bodies at the farm of another former manager. This all looks interesting. We have the bodies in our jurisdiction, but Goodson and the mill are county. The minute we identify a body that's from outside of Westwood, the state or Feds will take over."

Williamson let that sink in for a minute, then came back with what he often said when a case got heavy. "We're gonna need a bigger boat."

As Chief Sanchez returned to her desk, Williamson considered giving Mallard another update to tell him about the latest find, but he hesitated. The picture. The EPA files. What other loose ends are out there? What else can come back to haunt him or mess up the upcoming transfer? If things kept going downhill, Williamson thought he might have to make plans for himself. Mallard was supposed to have taken care of his end of cleaning up after Baker, and Williamson sure as hell took care of his. If the next couple of days kept getting worse, he'd have to call in a few favors from a few compatriots in Montana and Wyoming and make himself priority number one before Mallard's rickety house of cards came crashing down on top of all of them.

24

Back in my room, I undressed and took a quick, hot shower. Then, as per my personal SOP, I applied skin lotion. Over the years, the lotion and its application had become something of a routine. In my mind, it left a micro-shield between me and the world. My process of application from toe to head was almost hypnotic, yet another way to escape for a few moments. The money I saved on cheap coffee was reinvested in quality lotions, as our skin is the barrier that keeps us safe from the outer world and the ghosts that inhabit it.

The trick was to warm the lotion by vigorously rubbing your hands together. This allowed for a thinner spread and for the lotion to enter the skin more easily, especially when the pores are open after a warm bath or shower. Using the tips of my fingers, I started with my face, jawline, and neck, getting as close to the hairline as possible, leaving no space for the ghosts to enter. Rather than simply covering from the top down, I focused on my right side first. Then the left.

Using my left hand, I applied the warmed lotion to my right side as far as I could reach, making overlapping circles on my arm, chest, and side to avoid missed areas. Before moving on to the left side of my torso, I used both hands to apply the lotion to my right leg, with the same care, using overlapping circles. Then, both hands on the left leg before mirroring the actions on the left side of my torso with my right hand.

No, I don't know exactly when I first did this, and yes, I realize the process and the whole thinking behind it make me sound like a crazy person.

The next part of the healing and restoration regimen was watching nature documentaries on my iPad, especially those narrated by David Attenborough. In bed, with the bedside light on, I settled into the thin sheets and clicked on an episode about the polar caps. The visuals were stunning, as always, and Sir Attenborough's voice was vibrant yet soothing. Halfway through the third beer and the second episode, I knew I wouldn't last long.

"Deep in the recesses of this remote jungle canyon," Sir David Attenborough pronounced, "only the most dedicated bonding pairs will survive the coming seasonal changes. The male and female will take turns guarding the nest and the newly arrived chicks while the other ventures into the monsoon rains to find what scant fruit remains."

Dedicated bonding pairs. I hardly remembered what those feelings were like anymore. After Cassandra, a part of me died, never to return. I was no longer a dedicated partner helping to protect the nest. I was just a bird on a branch, sitting by myself, tolerating the monsoon. My female, my Laura, was left to gather fruit on her own. She had to protect the nest without a partner, but no newly hatched chicks would arrive.

Even in the dream, I could feel my longing for her. After almost a year of her begging me to get some help for whatever trauma she knew I must have experienced, she couldn't stay any longer. She said she had to leave, and I didn't have the strength to ask for help. No matter how much I loved her and wanted her, I was frozen in helplessness. But that was before.

I continued to sit alone on the branch in the monsoons until the estranged mate flew to me and sat on a nearby branch. She turned to me, and through the rain and wind, she yelled out, "All those people are dead—but you're not. You're alive. Do something about it!"

I woke at 5:30, headphones on, the bedside light still on, a drained iPad, five empty Budweiser bottles, a headache, and shame. Yet—there was a kernel of something inside—a purpose.

25

3 years earlier

Stadium Diner should have died twenty years ago. Tucked away in Leeds, a throwaway industrial area in the shadow of both Kauffman and Arrowhead stadiums, the diner rarely saw busy days. It only took cash; the menu hadn't changed for forty years, and it seemed like it had been that long since the grill hoods had been cleaned. Still, it stayed open all night, and they always had coffee going. The diner was where Warren would go to finish up the admin details of whatever his last call was, at least when he didn't leave a scene with a guest in the back seat.

He'd bring in his laptop, set a $5 bill on the counter, grab a mug, help himself to a cuppa, sit at one of the Atomic Age Formica tables that skirted the back and side walls, and get to work on whatever case he needed to wrap up before someone new died, was assaulted, had their feelings hurt, or needed to yell at a police officer about their own life's shortcomings. Tonight, when he came in, he nodded to Randall, the ancient black man who worked the grill between 11 pm and 6 am, and dove into his work.

About five minutes into work and coffee. Two truckers entered the diner and put Randall to work with two orders of burgers and fries. Several trucking companies had offices in the neighborhood, and the area was home to old rigs and trailers that had seen better days and would probably never see another day of action. These guys had probably recently finished a run and had secured their rig in one of the local yards for the night. This wasn't a place where drivers would park their trucks outside and sleep in them. That would be asking for trouble. There were enough late-night creepers, junkies, and ne'er-do-wells running around in the darkness that they would surely be rolled or have parts of their trucks stolen while they were sleeping.

After thirty minutes of work, Warren wrapped up his report and addenda on a minor case, backing up a patrolmate on a domestic violence arrest. The truckers had left, and the place was silent except for the radio playing oldies next to the grill. Warren drained the last of his coffee and filled up his thermos before departing. He grabbed his laptop and headed out, but not before a final, wordless wave to Randall. They'd see each other again in a few days. He had parked across the street from the diner and all the way west of it on the block. There was no traffic this time of night, and he could hear the light traffic on I-70 to the north.

As he left the front door of the diner, Warren crossed the sidewalk and went directly across the street to where an abandoned trailer was parked on the shoulder. It was darker on this side of the road, and he had more cover. Always seek cover, even when you don't think you'll need it—because you'll never know when you'll need it. Warren always had this mantra in mind. Just about every cop and soldier who ever patrolled did, too.

He walked in the shadows cast by the branches of the beech trees and the awnings of the buildings along the street. When he was about thirty feet from his vehicle, he pressed the unlock button on the key fob. Warren had opened the passenger-side door and set his laptop on the seat when three shots rang out.

Warren's body, like anyone's would, reacted to the situation with a massive jolt of adrenaline. How the body responds at this point can vary from person to person and from situation to situation. One might flee the perceived danger, freeze, or lash out in defense. For Warren, the reaction was a mix of the three, a calculated series of responses shaped by years of training and experience.

It was "go time!"

He crouched down next to his vehicle for some hasty cover. "City, Echo Paul 34! Shots fired!" he said calmly and quietly into the mic clipped to the upper left panel on his external vest.

"Go, Echo Paul 34," said the female-form automaton back in Dispatch.

"Three shots fired. Bennington Avenue south at Stadium Drive. No suspects, victims, or vehicles in sight. Approaching nearby intersection on foot to investigate further."

The dispatcher issued a call to other units in the area, and EP-72 responded, saying she was en route. Warren knew Officer Sheila Black was about nine minutes away, based on where she last showed up on the GPS tracker on the screen while in the cafe.

The southwest corner of Bennington and Stadium Drive held an old house whose best days had passed thirty years ago, and the shells of a dozen cars, trucks, and trailers whose time of use had long passed. There was a row of near-dead boxwoods along the property's western edge, but as soon as Warren passed those, he could see across the open, dead lawn area and down into Bennington Street a couple of hundred feet. He saw a dark SUV parked facing him along the opposite sidewalk, but nothing else of note. He continued east along Stadium Drive to see more of what might lie down Bennington. Down at the far end of the street, before it reached 39th Street, he saw the taillights of another vehicle making a left turn. The asphalt of 39th Street ended shortly after the turn, but several gravel roads ran between the truck yards and another along the sides of the Blue River. If the driver knew the area, he'd be able to find a way out of the cul-de-sacs and onto I-70 easily enough.

"City, Echo Paul 34," he said into the mic.

"Echo Paul 34, City. Go!"

Warren called in the meager vehicle description and its direction. He also told dispatch about the one SUV at the scene and gave the plate number as he approached.

Warren had been sweeping the beam of his Streamlight flashlight around the area, checking for other bodies or vehicles. Seeing none, he approached the car and shone his light on it. There was a body slumped over the steering wheel, and the driver's window was open. He called in the body's presence and approached further.

The body seemed lifeless, but he needed to check, so Warren pulled him back, revealing the gunshot wounds: one in the head, one in the throat, and two in the face, almost completely caving it in. There was plenty of blood, but none was actively leaving the body, indicating no heartbeat. There were also no gurgling noises, so no air was going in or out. Warren didn't feel the need to check for a pulse. Horrendous as the scene was, he couldn't look away for a full minute. It was both horrible and unavoidable.

Eventually, Warren collected himself and resumed his visual sweep of the area. There was no reason to leave the scene, but he circled the vehicle and stepped onto the sidewalk, shining his light into the old, long-abandoned storefronts that lined the street corner. What had once been a quaint neighborhood market area had long since become a quiet, dark place for shooting up or smoking whatever drugs one had.

As he made his way to the back of the vehicle, he shone his light into the SUV's back seat and cargo area. A leather case was on the floor in front of the rear passenger-side seat. It was black, shiny, and looked like a much larger version of an old doctor's travel bag. He knew he shouldn't disturb the scene, but Warren's curiosity got the better of him, partially because he already suspected what might be inside, and he opened the door to inspect the case. It had a hasp on it but no lock. Warren pushed the small button on the latch, and the teeth of the hasp opened.

Cash. Lots of it. Bundles of $20s and $100s.

The part of Warren's mind that had been looking for an escape from life flared to the forefront. In the past, that escape came to mind in heavy alcohol use, meaningless sex, and thoughts of abandoning life. Not so much suicide as simply lying down and not getting up. He had always worked through these bad thoughts, though, because he truly wanted to live a good life, one not full of death and yelling and bad smells. In fifteen seconds, the part of his brain that wanted to live formulated a complete plan—then forced Warren into action.

The area was abandoned; the businesses here had been closed for years. The house across the street had no known occupants, and there was no traffic in this area except for the diner patrons around the corner. Still, Warren had to act quickly.

He closed the latch on the bag and, after taking one last look around, grabbed it by its handle and went to the front door of one of the shuttered businesses in the building next to where the SUV sat. He tried the doorknob but didn't expect it to be open. It wasn't, but he made a calculated guess that he could pry off the piece of plywood covering the glassless window to the left of the door. The wooden covering was about two feet by four feet and looked like others had already pried it off. It had nails at its four corners, but when Warren began pulling at its side, only two of those nails were still securing the wood to the frame. He set the bag down, and with one smooth pull, the plywood came away cleanly from the frame without bending the nails much. As expected, the glass beneath had long disappeared, and Warren grabbed the case and stepped through the window into the store.

Shining his flashlight around, he saw a few shelves and racks that made him think this might have been a clothing store back in its day. There weren't any signs that anyone had been in here recently, but as the floor was littered with so much debris, peeled paint, fallen plaster, old papers of some kind, and mouse droppings, he couldn't see if there were any footprints. Above, he noticed several drop-ceiling tiles had fallen, revealing the rafters, wires, and old AC vents. Perfect!

Warren grabbed an old wooden chair that had survived here unmolested for so many years and dragged it to a spot underneath an opening in the ceiling near the rear right corner of the room. He placed the case in the opening onto the aluminum crossbars that held the tiles, then slid it back several feet. He grabbed a piece of the old insulation padding and wadded it up in front of the case to obscure it in case anyone stuck their head up the hole. It was the best he could come up with on such short notice.

He climbed off the chair and moved it back to where he had found it. Then he returned to the spot where the chair had been and moved the debris on the floor. Warren kept his light off and followed the brightness from the streetlamps as they shone through the glassless window he had entered. Before stepping through, he glanced around and listened for anyone in the area or vehicles arriving, but sensed nothing. He stepped through, grabbed the plywood, and set it back where it had been before he came. Using the butt of his flashlight, he hammered the nails back in the best he could and turned again to the scene.

Warren had stepped off the curb and into the street when a siren wailed in the distance. It sounded as if it was coming from the west. Probably Sheila, coming from Emanuel Cleaver II Boulevard. Coming fast, too. Warren's heart was racing, but there was nothing as he looked around again. No witnesses. No one except a dead guy in an SUV.

Officer Black arrived. She parked her vehicle on Bennington about 100 feet south of the victim's car. She walked briskly to Warren, and he brought her up to speed, telling her all his actions and observations, minus the details of the leather case and his blatant theft of it— just another crime scene in the City of Fountains. As Warren talked, Black popped her trunk and grabbed the roll of yellow "POLICE" tape, tied it at waist level to a post on the west side of the street, unrolled it, and tied it to the door handle of an abandoned building on the east side.

26 - Friday

5:30 was way too early to wake up after having so much to drink the night before. I got up to use the bathroom and brush my teeth, checked to make sure I had the laptop and phone plugged in to recharge, then lay down to try to get another batch of sleep. It worked partially. I drifted off now and then, but I couldn't get too comfortable with so much noise on the street outside. I had gotten used to the silence surrounding my place, so even the slightest bustle of this "big city" made me stir.

I checked the phone and saw that I had slept through a text from the chief.

Call me when you're up.

Though it wasn't the best quality sleep, it helped clear the fuzz from my head. I called the chief back. "What's up, Supe?"

Sanchez told me about the meeting at the mill and its staff, her visit to Lana Goodson's home, and what she found there. "I'm gonna head over to your place to get an update from the state team and check up on Pedersen and Langhorne. I got a text from them saying they're mostly wrapped up with the inside of your barn."

"They find anything good?" I knew the answer, but I wanted it to be "No."

"Yeah," Sanchez said in an almost apologetic tone. "They found a bunch of girls' stuff. Stuff you'd expect a guy like him to keep after he snuffed a gal. More restraints and such, as well as lots of papers, some personal and some from the mill. Knowing what I got from Lana, I'm curious to see what he had stored away about the mill. I haven't talked to Fuller about the body count, but I'll tell you when I know."

"What do you think of the connection between Gillum and Tracy? How does that fit into this?" I saw the peaks in the data, but not how they connected.

"I'm not sure yet. Let me go through what they found, and I may know more. Hey, do me a favor today."

"Sure," I replied. "I find myself without anything to do. What's up?"

"I'd like you to do some legwork for me. Online stuff." Sanchez used her patrol supervisor voice. "There are a couple sites that track and archive EPA violations. One is the official site, and another was set up by a watchdog group. Check to see what they have on there about Upriver, Mallard, or even Baker. I'll send you the links. It'll be a tedious search, and I'm gonna be running around all day. Can you handle that for me?"

"Yeah. Easy enough. Any word on when I can have my dirt back?" I asked hopefully.

"No, but I'll find out more when I'm there." Sanchez softened her tone. She knew I must be antsy as hell without my dirt and my girls. I'm sure she was pleased that I was holding it together this well. She didn't know about my bender last night, and I wasn't about to tell her.

At best, I hoped I'd be able to get my place back tonight, but that depended on the state crew and how far they'd gone through the land. I suspected Sanchez knew more about the body count than she let on, but I let it go.

I'd do it too, after breakfast. The Rathdrum didn't have a huge breakfast crowd, but almost a dozen patrons were there enjoying food and coffee. I got onto the same barstool that I had been on the night before.

"Good morning, Murphy," I said to Longman.

"Well, howdy," Murphy said. "You okay this morning? Last night you left here right as rain. You and Dan were getting along so well, I thought you'd start holding hands."

"I'm good. You caught me in a chatty mood last night." I was not too fond of that part of drinking, the part that makes nights foggy, the part that makes memories slip away. It meant I was far beyond the bounds of the behavior I wanted to exhibit. Sure, I didn't think of the bodies, the smells, or the sadness of the missing girls, but it also meant that I fell back into one of my old traps. I knew that I'd be in a different mood today. To compensate for the alcohol-induced fun and openness, I'd be extra tight today. Not mean or rude. Just tight. The kind of mood that Laura hated the most.

I ordered an omelet from the menu and asked for the coffee to keep flowing. I spent breakfast time hiding on my phone, sucking up more endorphins from the news and social media. I kept chit-chat to a minimum.

27

After finishing her conversation with Warren, the chief's next call was to Captain Petrelli to give an update. She left out any details about the mill. Since Fuller and his team worked for him, she assumed he knew about the body count, but updated him anyway.

"Fuller said this morning on the phone that he's up to nine bodies now, all in different states of decomposition," she said slowly. "I'll say it now so that you don't have to. I assume that at least one of these girls is going to turn out to be a resident of someplace other than Westwood, so I'm keeping my mission simple. We'll continue to secure the scene and collect and document all the evidence in the barn. I'm headed out there in a few to help my guys wrap up the collection. I'll make certain that we secure everything here at the station and that we have someone on the scene until Fuller is done."

Petrelli chuckled on the other end of the line. "I'm sure you will. We'll probably be doing the same thing, too. If even one of those girls is from out of state, we'll be handing this all over to the Feds. We'll be working for them. That's how it goes. I'm not worried about territories in this case. I'm sure that we all want to get the bodies identified so the families can rest easier."

Petrelli said his goodbyes abruptly, and Sanchez headed in her cruiser to Warren's place in her cruiser. The spring weather here was mercurial. It had been drizzling in the early morning, but enough clouds had since parted that the sun was bright and the air was warm. She was sure that it would change in a few minutes.

As she approached Warren's home, she saw COP Belzer getting out of the camping chair he had brought. He had added an umbrella and a cooler since her last visit. "Hello, Paul. Anything going on?" she asked.

Paul Belzer was a retired Spokane County sheriff's deputy who now lived in Westwood. He'd been off the force for almost fifteen years and had found that pure retirement didn't suit him. Still in his late sixties and active, he gave a couple of days a week to the county's Citizens on Patrol program. He did a variety of random tasks for any of the county's agencies. Today and yesterday were traffic control, except there was no traffic.

"No, Chief." He spoke slowly. He had plenty of time to kill, and there was no need to rush a conversation. "The only cars that have come by have been from the Powells up the road. Jim went out early to work, and Marilyn headed out an hour later for her job in Spokane Valley. Other than that, nothing."

"Well," she said back to him, just as slowly, "that may not be very exciting for you, but it's best if we don't have any gawkers. You have enough water? Need anything?" She liked the old cop. Every time they've chatted, he'd drop a nugget of wisdom either about police work in general or about the people in Westwood. He was a good guy to have around. Belzer said he was fine and, after a quick nod, returned to the shade and comfort of his chair and umbrella.

She parked her vehicle next to the state van and headed toward the barn. Fuller's team was on the far side of Warren's field, so she waved and continued into the barn. Pedersen and Langhorne had made fine work of the place. Near the main door she had just entered, they had piled several of the banker's boxes. Using the white evidence containers they had brought out, they'd gathered several boxes' worth of loose papers and folders scattered in different corners of the barn. She looked at the evidence-tracking sheet for each box and saw they were doing it correctly: vague descriptions of the papers and the area of the barn from which they were collected.

They had also created an impromptu photo area. Near the pile, they had laid a canvas tarp on the ground, and on top of that, Pedersen placed a four-foot-by-four-foot piece of white-painted plywood. Along the left side and bottom of the board were marks indicating inches and feet. When a stray piece of potential evidence was found, the officers placed it on the board and took a photo to verify its existence and size. They placed each item they gathered in a bag, plastic or paper, depending on what kind of object it was, then put it in another one of the white boxes for transport and further processing. It was tedious work, but the chief noted their progress.

She looked at Pedersen and asked, "So what's the creepiest thing you've found?"

Langhorn's face lit up because he knew what his partner would say. "Go check box number seven, in the paper bag," Pedersen said with a grin.

She didn't want to play along, but she did anyway. Number seven was where she expected, in the pile between six and eight. She lifted the lid and immediately saw the bag they meant. Three other items were bagged and placed in the box, but she was confident that the one on top was what they meant for her to see. Inside the brown paper bag was a doll. Unlike most dolls, this one was a boy doll. It had a hard plastic head, but the rest was of a soft, flannel-like material, and he had all his clothes removed. As if an old, naked doll wasn't creepy enough, Sanchez turned it over and saw what made this the clear winner. On the backside of the doll, where an anus would be, the soft material had been torn or cut, and inside of it was a desiccated human finger wearing what appeared to be an engagement ring.

"Yeah," the chief agreed. "That's pretty fucking creepy. You guys come across any paperwork from the mill or the EPA?"

"Yeah." Langhorne checked his clipboard quickly. "Box three."

Box three held a wide variety of items, all uniform in size, 8.5" x 11", so the contents were neat and easy to sort. Within a few moments, she found what she was hoping for—two folders from June 2007.

28

Athol lay in a flat, narrow stretch of Northern Idaho, where glaciers had carried rocks and boulders, carving the land over the past few hundred millennia. When the latest supereruption from the Yellowstone area occurred around 630,000 years ago, it produced enough rubble that, even this far west, earth and stone were blown into the paths of the slowly advancing glaciers. As the glaciers continued their gravity-driven march, the ice's power mixed with the debris, helping to create vast swaths of flat land. The stones in my fields are simply the crumbs of all that ruckus.

Today, though, I found nothing exciting about this part of the county: straight gravel roads, poorly managed stands of pine, ugly mobile homes, and the amusement park. I had planned to drive all the back roads in the area of the mill, but that had taken far less time than planned. Even with a stop for lunch at The Country Cafe and a quick walk around a hidden pond filled with snowmelt, I had far more time to kill than I would have liked. I decided to do some more exploration.

I pulled the CR-V into the gravel lot outside of the Upriver Mill. If I were going to do some research for the chief, I might as well get eyes on the place, too. I had my laptop with me, and after I got settled in between two truckless trailers in the lot, I pulled it out and searched for a signal from my phone. There was poor cell service here, only one bar, but I'd be fine if I stuck to text searches rather than video.

Before I could get too comfortable on the web, I spotted two trucks coming up the short road from the highway to the mill; both had dual trailers, and both were heavily loaded with long, slender tree trunks. I was pleased with myself for knowing the names of the grasses and wildflowers on my land, but I hadn't gotten around to learning all the trees yet. If I had to guess, these were western white pines, but I wasn't sure.

As the trucks passed, I saw they both had British Columbia plates, and neither had a sleeper cabin. They were probably doing straight runs from the felling site to here. If these logs were to become pulp for stove pellets, there was no use in curing them at a lumber yard first. The trucks continued into the mill's fenced area and came to a stop, one behind the other, next to the scale. I didn't hear them honk, but soon after they arrived, I saw a man step out of the main building and head toward the truck. One by one, he went to the driver's door, checked some papers, and directed them onto the scales. First one truck, then the other, went on and off the scale, then wound around an already impressive pile of logs and deeper into the lot. The man came out of the scale house and over to an ancient track-wheeled crane in the lot. Soon, it too went around the corner.

I couldn't see where they went, but my curiosity was piqued. What little boy doesn't enjoy seeing Tonka toys in action? I looked around the parking lot again but saw no one else, so I left the car and walked toward the chain-link fence south of the entrance. I had to walk a couple hundred feet along the fence before the rows of stored logs opened up, giving me a view of the trucks and the loader tank. About 200 feet into the yard, the workers gathered at the end of one of the log rows with the trailers lined up behind each other. Standing away from his vehicle, the driver of the first truck watched as the mill employee with the crane unloaded the logs, a dozen at a time. The crane arm would come down with its two claws and grasp up enough weight to crush any man, raise ten feet above the height of the load, swivel it around, and drop the logs as neatly as could be onto the existing pile. How many tons had this guy moved over the years?

With four trailers full of logs, I knew this would take a while to unload. I didn't see any other activity in the lot, the yard, or near the office, so I took a walk around the mill to see what the different parts looked like and how big it was. It was close to the interstate and a modestly busy county road. I could hear the traffic, but I couldn't see it. Walking around the fenced lot, I saw rows and rows of the same type of trees. Most looked like they had recently arrived, but the stacks in the far reaches of the lot appeared more aged, as if they might have wintered over.

On the far side of the mill, a small, mostly ignored road ran toward an equally unused gate in the fence. I was careful to stay out of the view of the three men in the lot and anyone who might be in the office, but there was no activity in the mill portion of the yard, nothing at all. It looked like a huge, three-story, three-sided shed. I couldn't tell what the various implements were used for inside, but its layout let me imagine trucks backing up to load and unload. I took out my phone, opened the camera app, zoomed in, and took a photo of the odd-looking building. In doing so, I noticed I didn't have cell service on this side of the mill. I'd pick someone's brain about how a mill works later.

Finishing my loop around the yard, I saw no other activity, but I heard the crane still working and went to the spot along the fence where I could see them again to check their progress. The fourth trailer was almost empty, so I headed back to my car. Within five minutes, the trucks lined up at the scale again and got weighed by the crane operator. The man made a few notes on each driver's clipboard, and the drivers signed a few items on the mill employee's clipboard. A few last words, and both trucks were back on the road, headed north for another load.

Back in my car, I began searching for the EPA website the chief had given me. Progress was slow due to poor service, but I eventually found it. After some trial and error, I came across an impressive list of low-grade complaints against the mill, dating from 2002 to 2013. Many complaints were closed soon after they were opened, but a couple from the early '00s carried significant penalties. In 2003, there was a $30,000 penalty for "COMPLIANCE FAILURE - Implementation Plan for National Primary and Secondary Ambient Air Quality Standards," and another in 2004. That one had a $50,000 penalty for what was listed as "Effluent Limit Violations Not Otherwise Specified, Violation Of A Permit Requirement, Violation Of Req. To Monitor/Maintain Records, Violations Of Reporting Requirements."

As this is a government website, I was hoping for a glossary or a list of definitions, but there were none. Also, in the "Additional Documents" tab, there were no annotations or files, but there was a case summary:

On September 09, 2004, Region 10 filed a consent agreement and final order resolving violations of the Clean Water Act by Upriver Paper Mill in Athol, Idaho. Respondent, which operates a lumber mill and depot and sells lumber and timber by-products, failed to follow prescribed conditions of the EPA Stormwater Multi-Sector General Permit, including Stormwater Pollution Prevention Plan deficiencies, failures to monitor, and failures to review control measures or add corrective actions. The company reported that the inspection and subsequent enforcement action led to improvements in compliance across all branches. At the Athol facility, the company switched from bi-monthly to semi-annual slurry operations, reducing toxic effluents to a compliant level and lowering concentrations of other metals and toxins in the facility's industrial stormwater runoff. The company agreed to pay a $48,508 penalty.

There were fourteen complaints against the mill during that period, but only those two led to significant penalties. Four of the remaining complaints were filed between 2005 and 2010 and carried much smaller fines because they involved self-reporting violations. The rest, starting in 2010, were all closed without fines or penalties. They didn't even list what the offense might have been.

I downloaded the report as a PDF, which took forever, and made a mental note to send it to the chief, along with a link to the search results. I was certain she could find more by comparing it with the reports she had found in the girl's closet.

Another rig pulled onto the road to the mill and caught my eye. I'd been out here long enough to get the lay of the land and had planned to head back to town, but I could delay it for a few minutes to see if this truck did the same thing. It was a sleeper rig, much bigger than the previous ones, but like those two, it was also from Canada and had two trailers full of thin logs, each probably sixteen feet long.

When the truck pulled into the yard, two men came out of the office: the one from before and an older man dressed for an office setting rather than a log yard. The truck pulled closer to the building than the other two had earlier, and the scale/crane operator from before came over to the driver's door and chatted right away. The older man didn't come to the truck. Instead, he went to the far side of the building, out of view for a few moments. Just after the log truck headed toward the unloading spot that the first man directed them toward, the second man came from behind the building, behind the wheel of a flatbed truck, a Ford F350 by the looks of it. Since moving to Idaho, I have seen hundreds of trucks like this, but unlike back in Kansas City, where I saw men driving them for ego gratification, here they are put to good use. Few of the trucks here were shiny. They were dirty and dented, rusted, and well-worn. The office man followed the log truck, and when the bigger one stopped near the crane, the flatbed pulled up alongside.

"Why the second truck?" I asked aloud. I stepped out of my vehicle and returned to the spot along the fence line to get a better look at the unloading.

Two sturdy metal bars alongside each trailer held the logs in place on the truck, but three wide canvas straps anchored on both sides of the trailer also helped. The driver and passenger got out as soon as they stopped, then loosened and removed the straps so the crane could do its job. It took four minutes to get them all off, but once clear, the crane claw began grabbing the logs from the bed of the first trailer.

Had there been no second truck, I might have just left, but I was curious what it was for. After working its way through the top of the pile and after three loads, its actions changed. Instead of picking up a claw full of logs, the operator deftly picked up one log at a time and moved to the side of the trailer. On the side near the second truck, one log shifted and slid down, but the metal support bar stopped it easily.

On a signal from the crane operator, the passenger of the log truck climbed into the bed of the trailer and scrambled on top of the logs until he came to the center of the load. There, he reached into the pile with one hand and motioned the claw down with the other. When the claw was a few feet above him, he pulled up a short chain and secured it to the claw. After taking a step back and using the visual shorthand he had learned over years of fieldwork, he motioned for the claw to rise slowly. With his eyes still on whatever was in the trailer, he extended his right hand, palm up, toward the crane operator and made short upward movements with his hand. As the claw rose, I could see more.

The chain was attached to other chains that secured a pallet that had been inside the pile of logs. The pallet was narrow, probably three feet by eight feet, and had a load on it. I couldn't see what it was as a white canvas tarp covered it on all sides. After the pallet cleared the top of the pile, the man onboard waved his hand as if shooing away a fly. This, the international symbol for "bring it up," was obeyed, and the claw began a slightly faster climb. It paused long enough for the man to scramble down, and as soon as he was clear of the trailer, the claw began toward the flatbed. As it got close, the driver of the log truck was there to guide the pallet in the right direction for the final descent.

The load hit the truck bed, and I could see its effect. The vehicle sagged but quickly bounced back. A few hundred pounds was nothing for a work beast like that. No one bothered to secure the load, but as soon as it was in, the older man said his goodbyes to the log truckers, drove the Ford back toward the office, and left the three to finish unloading.

29

I walked back toward the gate, trying to stay out of sight while also trying to see where the truck had gone. It wasn't parked outside, and I couldn't see it under the cover of any mill buildings. I assumed there was a garage or shed on the other side of the office building that I hadn't seen. I returned to my car and wanted to leave, but I was pretty sure the men in the yard would notice the commotion. Instead, I gambled with the cell service and gave Sanchez a call. My first two attempts failed, but on my third, I got a call through.

"I'm busy!" Sanchez said, sounding extra tinny and choppy because of the weak signal. "I'm going through the boxes from your barn. Enough shit in here to keep us both in therapy for years. What's up?"

"Okay, Supe. I'll be quick." I used my clipped, efficient, report-making voice. "I've been sitting by the mill for a couple hours watching how it works. Very little activity here. Only two employees that I can see, and only three deliveries today. Two seemed normal, logs from Canada. The third delivery was different."

"Different how?" she asked.

"Different in that during the unloading of the logs, they also pulled out a pallet of something that had been hidden inside the pile. I didn't see what it was, but as soon as they got it out, they secured it somewhere on the property."

Silence on the phone. Just like when I saw the transfer, Sanchez was now going over some possibilities about what might be happening. Drugs were the obvious answer, but that didn't mix with the EPA stuff. She had seen the reports I sent, but I didn't think either of us knew how the two threads weaved together yet. It was her turn to share.

"We found the missing EPA reports in your barn." Now, the chief used her information-relaying voice. "Baker had them in one of the boxes in there. At this point, I'm running with the idea that Goodson was trying to blackmail him or Mallard, but Baker put a stop to that. He killed her and took the documents back, thinking that's all she had."

"Yeah," I added, "that sounds right, but what does this load have to do with all that?"

"I don't know. It could be a lot of things, but there's no reason for a warrant for the mill at this point. I'll ask, but don't have high hopes. We're gonna follow this EPA trail for now, but we'll probably have to turn it all over to State or Feds by the end of the day." Sanchez wasn't happy about this, and I could hear it in her voice. "So far, there are nine bodies found at your place, and we have no idea how they fit in other than Goodson. Get out of there, come back to the hotel, and we'll meet up in a bit."

"Got it. Out." It was shocking yet comforting how easily I went back into RoboCop mode when the right stimulus was there. Sanchez and I worked together so very well when it mattered.

I waited about five minutes after the now-empty log truck left the yard, and the crane operator went back into the building before I pulled out from my spot. I was equally careful as I pulled back onto the main road.

The Stone Harvest

Looking both ways twice to make certain that no one was there to see me enter the highway from the mill road, I headed back to Westwood.

30

Williamson stood placidly as he and Detective Oliveira listened to the chief on the phone with Warren. The three had been reviewing the papers that Langhorne and Pedersen had found in Cha's barn. He had hoped that if he found something interesting, he could get rid of it before the chief saw it, but that didn't work out. She found the EPA reports before he could. Instead, he helped her make copies of them and fill in the missing months of the files in Goodson's closet. He was helping to nail his own coffin, and he didn't like it one single bit.

He wasn't sure if the chief had yet put it together, but he knew. Since 2003, Mallard and Baker had kept two sets of self-inspection records for the EPA. The fines they had paid in previous years had weakened the mill, already close to death, but Mallard didn't want to give up. Instead, he and Baker bribed and threatened whoever they needed to keep the books looking good and the EPA out of their way. In addition, they found new revenue streams and uses for the mill. The Ukrainians saved the mill as much as anyone else, and Mallard wanted to nurture that connection, not only for the income. The loss of life if they were upset seemed a real possibility, too.

He never knew exactly what Cha did with Goodson. He just knew she had disappeared after making some noise to Gillum about blackmail. How fucking stupid of the old man to get rid of the girls on

153

his own property, he thought. Then again, the secret held all these years long enough for Cha to live out his life. Not so good for the rest of us now. Williamson had suspicions about Cha and other missing girls, but he had no idea how active he had been. Cha must have acquired a taste for killing somewhere along the line, and he did an excellent job of keeping it a secret—and hiding the bodies.

Williamson didn't like what he was picking up from the phone call. Apparently, Warren had been at the mill and saw part of a delivery, but couldn't see enough to convince the chief to rush in or get a warrant. He knew the chief had enough information to connect the mill, the dead girl, and Baker, but didn't think she had put the drug shipments in the mix. *That fucking prick!* He thought with a passive face. This new information might change that.

When the chief hung up with Warren, she headed to her office and picked up her phone. She shut her door so that Williamson couldn't hear who she was talking to. He excused himself from the table without a word and stepped out the back door to the parking lot. He stood in a spot where he knew the cameras wouldn't see him and pulled out his phone to call Mallard.

31

Mallard slumped in his home office chair after hearing Quint's update. He hated the news, but this is why he kept the old cop on retainer. Dropping so much money over the years had sometimes been a stretch on his budget, and he rarely used it, but when he did, it was for big-deal events like this.

He knew they could eliminate proof of almost any dirt between Baker and the mill, and he was confident that they could eliminate any trace of the second set of inspection records. Because they hadn't been doing nearly as much actual millwork as in the past, any spot inspection wouldn't yield much: a few penalties for missing records, maybe some minor infractions for effluent and airborne waste, but nothing fatal.

The big transfer had to go on tomorrow. Too much money and product were at stake. They had to get the product out of here, out of the mill, and he sure as hell needed that money to pay off the Ukrainians. He needed until tomorrow afternoon. They could fix the rest later. For now, he needed Warren out of the way.

Mallard recalled several summers earlier, when two of his yard crew were drawing too much attention from the Sheriff's Department because of their scrapes with the law. They had been arrested for low-level dealing, and deputies were giving them plenty of attention, even visiting the mill twice to serve search warrants on their vehicles. Concerned that this might interfere with the monthly transfer, Mallard called the

Ukrainian "family" in the North, explained the situation, and asked whether it would be all right for him to call his southern half and delay the pickup by a couple of days.

The slightly accented voice on the phone of the man they knew only as "Uncle" was calm and sympathetic, but would not allow such a thing. Instead, he asked for the names of the two men, both long-time mill employees. Within a day, one of them had been found dead of an accidental heroin overdose in a Spokane shoot house, and the other called from outside Phoenix, saying that he wasn't coming back. So, no, delaying a transfer was not a viable option.

Upsetting either the Ukrainians from the Great White North or the Irishmen from Kansas City seemed like a poor choice, and it was that way from the beginning of this arrangement, an arrangement that popped up at the perfect time. It came ten years ago, when Mallard and the mill were at their lowest financial and legal point, with few contracts, little capital on hand, low pulp and timber prices, and Mallard overextended by gambling debts.

Mallard loved betting on college football, but he was as bad at it as he was at running a mill. As his debts from his losses mounted, what saved him from physical harm was his bookie's ability to sniff out a good opportunity.

Del Hood, known to Kootenai County authorities as Delbert Huddington, had Mallard in his pocket for $15,000. That was a big enough problem for both parties, but Del Hood owed his supplier and loan agent in Kansas City, Reardon, almost $35,000.

In one of their chats, Reardon said that he needed a quiet transfer point to meet his Ukrainian-Canadian friends. Mallard's mill met all the requirements: private yard, close to the highway and border crossing, all equipment needed for loading and transfer, and secure storage. Del Hood set up Reardon's end, and Reardon called the Ukrainians to get them the location information and details.

In the first year, on the day of any deliveries or transfers, Mallard and Baker cleared the lot of employees and handled every aspect of the transfer themselves. The drivers from the north started as a rotating cast but soon settled into a regular team, whereas Del had been on hand from day one to receive the shipment from the mill and make the payment. He'd never missed a month in all the years of doing this. Mallard had to admire that consistency.

He preferred working from home rather than at Upriver. It wasn't as if he had to prove himself able to do any of the work required at a mill, as he'd been working that machinery for years. It's just that the phone and computer are his most-used tools now. The chair here was more comfortable, the place was warmer, and there was always bourbon. It was always peaceful at home—most of the time.

Gerald Mallard found himself in a real predicament with Karl Warren, but fortunately, two Canadian tools had recently arrived for him. This wasn't a situation Quint could solve, and Gillum simply lacked the powers of persuasion, threats, or bribery that Cha had.

He picked up his phone.

The Stone Harvest

"I have a small problem with a chicken farmer. How would you guys like to make five hundred apiece?"

32

PTSD is a tricky snake to wrestle.

It took me several years to discover or acknowledge that it was even a thing. For the longest time, I thought I was hyper-alert or maybe simply an asshole. Then, as soon as the condition entered my lexicon through post-incident counseling after a particularly gruesome auto fatality, it gave me some boundaries for what a healthy personality and behavior could or should be. Shortly after that, through some reading I did on my own, I began to see some of my coping mechanisms: drinking, seclusion, and a quick temper.

The best thing that happened during this learning phase was discovering my triggers. I had seen fireworks displays several times in those years. While I put on a happy face for my friends or Laura, I always spent the duration in an agitated state. I'd spend the next day in a recovery phase, effectively shutting myself off from the world. If on those days I had to work or be with Laura, I would be by turns sullen, quick to temper, then quiet again. It may not seem like much to an outsider, but those roller coasters were hell on the relationship.

Fourth of July celebrations were definitely not on my things-to-see list anymore. Idaho is one of those states that not only allows fireworks to be sold freely but also seems to make it a mandatory social ritual to blow up as much stuff as possible during the holiday celebrating freedom. My home was far enough from town and popular hangouts that as long as I stuck to my place, my sanctuary during the Fourth, I'd be fine.

There were other triggers, too. Some were quite innocuous. An unexpected car horn or a patrol partner hitting their siren unexpectedly. Also, the deep bass from the speakers of a passing car or, embarrassingly, when one of the neighbors' kids would sneak up and try to scare me. In each case, the noise or shock was like a tiny needle prick to my brain. Yes, I could immediately recognize the "threat" for what it was, but the damage would be done. The heart rate would spike, adrenaline would pump, and I'd be hyper-alert for several hours afterward. The next day, the body would recover from that stress by shutting down emotionally. I'd go back into my mental cave and be a robot to those around me. Sure, I'd put on my public face, but it would be an act, a mask. In the past several years, I had lost count of the days I had been in this autopilot mode.

I returned to The Rathdrum Inn after the last of the day's light and found a spot at the bar in the far corner. I had a lot to unpack from today mentally, and couldn't quite stomach the idea of sitting alone in my room yet. From this perch, I couldn't see the west side of the bar that held the games and the dance floor, but I had the door covered, as always. A couple of locals were sharing a pitcher of beer along the far wall while shooting pool on the slightly crooked table. Neither set off any alarm bells, but one of them paid more attention to me than normal. Just an overly long glance, but it was enough to get on my radar.

Murphy came out of his office at the same time that I sat down. Its door was down the hallway from the restrooms, closest to the exit to the back lot.

"Hey, stranger. What you been up to today?" the large bartender said as he approached me from behind.

"Not much at all. Took a long drive up north to see a few roads I hadn't traveled yet. It's nice up there. Jack and Coke, please."

He made the drink, ice water, too, and we exchanged more pleasantries. Murphy removed an empty pint glass from the bar, then returned to his office to wrap up whatever he was doing.

Recalling the chat with the chief, I could put most of the picture together, but now, as she said, there's not enough for a warrant and no clear path ahead yet. With the stir stick in the drink, I made circles with the ice in my nearly empty glass. Perhaps the more I spun it, the quicker a solution would appear. All of this is headed to the Feds in a matter of days anyway, so no use getting too—

CRACK!

Within a second, I had diagnosed the sound and its source, but the damage was done. I knew a couple of fellas were shooting pool on the other side of the bar, but I never imagined the sound of the initial rack break could be so loud—or such a trigger. This one didn't require any breathing to remedy it, nor did it put me into as much of an adrenaline high as a bigger trigger would, but it certainly caught my brain's attention.

Though I recognized the sound for what it was, I sat more rigidly on the stool than usual, letting my brain cycle through the brief shock and its chemical aftermath. Often, if the shock from a trigger is big enough, the next phase would be a mild withdrawal from the world, and when back in a safe space, such as home, a full-on depression would come on the scene. With such a mild one, though, it brought a sense of vigilance, a hyper-awareness. My brain didn't want to be caught by surprise again, so it pumped out enough energy and adrenaline to ensure it wouldn't happen again tonight. Perhaps that's an understandable reaction, but an awfully inconvenient one. I wouldn't be able to turn my mind off and fall asleep for several hours.

I got off the barstool and headed down the hallway to the restroom. On my way in, I called out, "Hey, Murphy! Another drink when you get a sec."

"Can do, Karl. Be waiting for you when you're back," he yelled through his open door.

The human brain is funny, especially when on a self-induced, chemically based high alert. It is capable of all manner of self-delusion in its lows, but when heightened, it can be a thing of wonder, forming spectacularly intricate deductions and computations from the few facts presented, weaving them into prior knowledge and experience. Those thoughts come at high volume and at high speed.

Upon finishing my business in the men's room, I opened the door and froze. Within the first half-second, I had already taken a complete inventory of the situation. Flannel was the bigger, stronger, and younger of the two, and as soon as we locked eyes, he tensed up, moved his feet into a boxer's stance, and balled up both hands into fists. He was about eight feet away from the back doorway, with Murphy's open office door between. My sudden appearance caught his partner, Tuxedo, off guard, and his face showed it. When he saw me open the bathroom door, he stepped back and stopped in line with the door marked "Ladies."

Flannel, off to my left, stood tall, maybe even leaning forward slightly, while Tuxedo, after composing himself, spoke firmly, "You've been asking about the mill, huh? Let's step outside and talk about it."

I secretly hoped that all they wanted to do was talk, but too many years of talking to too many tough guys made me pretty certain there'd be little talking involved. I hadn't been in a fight or any altercation for about two years: nothing but yoga and an occasional Krav Maga session in Spokane to keep in tune. I was slightly out of shape, my martial skills were rusty, and their appearance took me by surprise. My alertness level was higher than usual because of the micro-trigger of the billiard balls cracking, but I still wasn't anywhere close to 100% ready for a brawl. I needed time and space.

"How 'bout we go talk at the bar? I'll buy you a beer," I offered. There was still a slim chance they did only want to talk about the mill. Maybe they could volunteer a few details about the place.

"How 'bout you move your ass outside so we can talk properly? Move it!" Tuxedo said, pointing to the back door. Flannel took a tiny step forward. That was the time and space that I needed.

In hindsight, I was confident I had done the right thing. Yes, I could have gone outside to "chat." I could have forced the issue and tried to walk back to the bar. The guys sure didn't want any public brawl, and I had seen the cameras in the bar, assumed they worked, and knew what they'd capture would create some public record.

I also knew that I was so full of angst and dread and remorse and frustration from all the goddamn dead bodies in my paradise. I knew that, should this come to a court hearing, I could easily verbalize that these two men had me in a vulnerable situation. Flannel's final step toward me made me sure I needed to act in self-defense to protect myself, your Honor. Also, I knew that I was gonna enjoy the hell out of this!

I made a rough calculation of the distance and acted quickly. Flannel was too big and too close to attack first effectively, so I directed my initial move toward Tuxedo. I moved my right foot between and slightly behind Tuxedo's legs, shuffled my left ten inches in front of and centered on him, and bent my left leg, keeping it tense. This allowed me to use my upper-body movement to lean in close to Tuxedo. With bent elbows, I put my palms flat on Tuxedo's upper chest and, in one motion, pushed with full strength against my left leg while extending it, used my right foot as a fulcrum to make Tuxedo lean back further, then, using the full force of my upper body, pushed hard while extending my arms. This collection of actions, committed in less than a second, sent Tuxedo flying backward into the same stool I had formerly occupied.

The action surprised Flannel. I was counting on that. With my right foot now planted, I whipped my head around to target the next blow. I saw Flannel hauling his right hand back for a big haymaker—a dangerous move in a tight hallway.

A baseball pitcher's fastball doesn't begin with the hand that the ball is in. It begins with the opposite hip. The pitcher will start his throwing motion by getting the opposite hip moving toward the plate. Then, the opposite knee, elbow, and foot. Then he begins with the throwing side; even so, the ball comes last. The pitcher flings his pitching shoulder forward. The physics of human anatomy will make the elbow follow; only then does the hand with the ball come into play. It's the exact engineering science as throwing a punch—or a forearm.

My head was already facing Flannel. In one movement, I bent my right knee and put all my weight on it, then opened my left hip by bringing my left leg and foot into line with my right toward Flannel. While my lower body danced, my left shoulder swung to the left, and the right shoulder followed suit. Pushing off firmly from my cocked right leg, I applied extra force to the rotation with my shoulder movement, but at no time did my eyes ever leave the target, the bridge of Flannel's nose. I was most of the way through this twist, and the push from my right leg got me square to the target. I raised my left forearm vertically to deflect Flannel's haymaker if he got it there more quickly than I thought he could. From where it began, outstretched after throwing Tuxedo across the room, my right elbow traveled about six feet from there, into the twisting transition movement, and then into the exact center of my target's face. Coincidentally, the sound of the impact was similar to that of a fastball hitting the catcher's mitt.

Flannel flew back and down through the rear door, but I didn't have time to enjoy the show. Tuxedo was

165

down, but only for a moment. I quickly swiveled to my right and toward the heap of a mess near my barstool. As he got off the floor, Tuxedo stuck his right hand into the left side of his waistband to bring out the Judge, a Taurus .45 that I'm sure served as his substitute cock whenever manhood issues arose. Perhaps it usually served him well, but not today.

I saw the action and what Tuxedo was reaching for, so I sprang forward and gripped his wrist with both hands before the weapon cleared his belt. Size matters, and I had the advantage here. In one smooth motion, I pulled the gun and Tuxedo's wrist straight up and slightly to my left. This brought the weapon straight up, and, after sliding my right hand near his elbow, it gave me the freedom to place my right elbow on the left side of Tuxedo's throat. I did so with plenty of pressure, enough to make its presence known, but not so much as to stop blood and oxygen from reaching the man's brain.

Time froze.

The brass rail of the bar pressed up against Tuxedo's upper back, and his hips and legs stayed further out and off-balance because of the barstool that I had been sitting on until recently. My height and weight pressed down firmly on his throat, and my two stronger, longer arms pulled his right arm to its full length. His left arm was free but could only swing in weak, impotent arcs toward the back of my right shoulder. The man was well and truly fucked.

I kept unwavering eye contact but pulled my right hand further up to cradle the Judge.

"Let go," I hissed to my new friend. Tuxedo complied. I returned my right elbow to the throat and gently set the Judge onto the bartop, but first I used my thumb to release the cylinder lock and dumped the six cartridges into the glass of water I never got to drink. I looked at Murphy, frozen behind the bar.

"Call the police, please." The barkeep complied.

After seeing Murphy on the phone with the police, I quickly reversed the grip of my right hand and placed it on Tuxedo's right wrist. With the grace of a 235-pound ballerina, I swung my right foot and hip in a clockwise arc to find a place to plant three feet directly in front of the suspended man. In another lightning-fast move, I pulled my hands down, along with Tuxedo's wrists, in a straight line to my right knee. This brought the bulk of his upper body down toward the floor, and as it passed my wrists, gave another slight twist to bring the man's right wrist behind his body so that he could land fully on his face. The impact was loud and wet.

As he did so, I brought the wrist behind Tuxedo's back as his weight fully hit the floor. The last move was to extend the man's wrist high into the air again while bringing my right knee to the back of Tuxedo's head. I firmly placed my left knee in the middle of his back, trapping Tuxedo's arm between my thighs. The prostrate man was now helpless, at my will.

The fight was over, but the adrenaline was still flowing. At this point, all I could do was enjoy the victory and breathe my way through the chemical aftermath. As I kneeled there, I monitored the rear door. Flannel peeked his head through, read the scene, and disappeared for good. I was left with a limp lumberjack between my thighs. I didn't spot any secondary threats, but I noticed that the one yokel that I'd noticed earlier shifted his cue to his off-hand, reached for his phone, and appeared to send a quick text.

33

Longman was behind the bar, making Warren's drink, when two men came in through the back door, entered, stood, and looked around as if searching for someone. He'd seen this a thousand times before: a man or woman looking for an early-arriving date, a co-worker looking for another, a jealous spouse trying to find a potentially philandering partner. He'd seen it all, but these guys had an edge to them. Neither looked particularly threatening if you listed their characteristics. Still, if you added up all that, plus their fast pace, elevated sense of urgency, and general disinterest in anything to do with the bar itself, Longman got a bad feeling about the two. The man in front, wearing the full Canadian tuxedo of jeans, an untucked denim shirt, and steel-toed boots, held his phone out to read a text that had popped up.

* * *

In the bathroom

Tuxedo showed the text to his less formal friend in the red flannel shirt. They both turned and headed down the hallway to the men's room door, with Tuxedo stopping before the door and Flannel taking two extra steps to stand on the other side. The two weren't trained brawlers by any definition, but they'd been in enough bar fights and scrapes together over the past few years that they thought, as a team, they could take on and rough up any single guy. Especially some chicken wrangler causing trouble for the mill and their cushy situation. Throw in $500, and it was an easy yes when Mallard called and made the offer. He had just turned his back to the exit when the restroom door opened, and Warren appeared. Tuxedo froze. This was the toughest-looking chicken wrangler he had ever seen. He needed a moment to think, but it all went downhill quickly from there.

* * *

After Warren's victory and Longman's call to the police, Williamson arrived in less than a minute. The flashing blue lights from his patrol vehicle weren't visible through the two small windows on the front side of the building because he had run from the station when the call came in. In hindsight, Williamson was slightly worried about a rebuke from the chief for violating protocol by leaving his vehicle behind. The reasoning was that the vehicle carried all the emergency equipment and the shotgun, and it was a better way to transport a prisoner, even though the station was only a few yards away. He'd live with the risk of a rebuke.

Williamson was pretty sure the scene was calm before he entered, but he played it safe, moving slowly and cautiously. He saw the locals in the back corner playing pool, Longman standing behind the bar looking nervous, and the chief's buddy giving the Thighmaster to a man on the ground. Warren looked quite comfortable sitting there. He should. That restraint position allowed maximum control of a subject with minimum effort. Once a subject was on the floor and under control, the officer didn't need to use his hands. A tiny squeeze of the thighs caused considerable discomfort, pain that never left a bruise on the subject—another benefit to law enforcement.

Warren's hands rested calmly on his thighs when Williamson came in. He lifted his hands to be clearly visible, letting Williamson know he had no weapon.

"There's an unloaded handgun on the bar. No others as far as I can tell," Warren told the officer. "And—could you call Charlie One and ask her to roll this way?" He said the last part sheepishly.

* * *

Longman thought this was one of the few times he wished Trapper Dan were here to see this brawl. Warren was impressive as hell, and the old barman worried he wouldn't be able to do the story justice.

* * *

Outside in the rear parking lot, Flannel had recovered from the initial shock and pain of Warren's assault enough to know that he was in trouble. He stuck his head inside the rear door to gauge the situation, not thirty seconds after he had flown through it, and what he saw let him know that the night was over. Warren was straddling his friend, and the barman was on the phone, presumably to the police. None of this looked good to him. He was lucky enough to have the keys to the truck they had borrowed from Mallard's lot, so he jumped in, started it up, and disappeared into the cool Westwood night.

34

Officer Miles Long arrived on the scene minutes after Williamson, and things got into high gear. Together, they interviewed the patrons, and of course, no one saw anything. Murphy, though, saw everything and gave a clearly detailed eyewitness account of the whole thing. After telling his story, he pulled Long into his office to show him the digital video of the fight. Above his desk, Murphy had a monitor that showed the camera feeds from the front door, the bar, the dance floor, the hallway, and the back lot. He downloaded the video from when the two guys walked in through the back door until Williamson came in through the front.

Sanchez got the message from Long that Warren was involved in the altercation, but she didn't go to the scene. Instead, she pulled into the station, knowing that Warren would be brought there for his statement. The chief had to let this play out for a while longer. She had heard enough details of the fight to be sure that Warren would be in the clear, but she had to let the others take the lead on this one.

It was after business hours, so there were no admin folks in the building. "Damnit! Make some more coffee if you take the last pot!" the chief yelled aloud at no one. *Probably Williamson*, she thought. She knew he and the team would be in the house for a while, so she wanted some coffee, but none was to be had. She made a fresh pot and headed to her office.

Once there, she flipped the switch for the house audio so she could listen to the police radio. She heard Williamson call for a records and warrants check on the men, the yokels. She didn't know the first one, but the other was a well-known problem child in town. Not a hardcore criminal, just a low-grade troublemaker and all-around punk. The coffee should've been ready by now, so Sanchez headed back to the mini-kitchen to grab a cup. On her way back, she passed the desk Williamson had used. Patrol officers, even sergeants, didn't get their own desks, but they used regular spots. This chair, close to the aisle and the chief's office, was where Williamson liked to sit.

In his rush to get to the scene at the bar, Williamson left some things behind: a couple of evidence tags from a case earlier in the shift and a still-warm cup of coffee.

Fucker! I knew it!

He had also left his smartphone, which she noticed when it buzzed again. The display was locked, but the sender's number and part of the message were visible on the screen.

"Call me as soon as..." was all she could read.

Sanchez returned to her desk and worked on the case. She'd often listen to a scene and do legwork on those involved. For this fight, she pulled up Warren's NCIC file. It was clean, of course. Murphy's showed that he had an interesting young adulthood, but no legal troubles since. The guy whom Warren bested was a Canadian with no record in the U.S. For information about the guy's Canadian record, she'd have to make a request through the state. That'll come tomorrow.

The yokels were quite a pair. Each had short of a dozen arrests or convictions for a variety of low-grade crimes: fraud, possession, possession with intent to sell, assault, DUI, and drunk in public. Winners both, but one of them, Rory David, was a local. His most recent police contact was for drinking in public on the day of the town's annual festival, Westwood Days. The other's record showed he lived in Spokane Valley, over the border to the west. The chief had been here three years and had seen David on several occasions, never to arrest him, but the guy seemed to be on the outskirts of all the bar fights and drug busts in town. Sanchez pulled up his file and saw David's phone number on record.

A wave of nausea rode through the chief. She had seen that number on the screen of Williamson's phone. Sanchez got up and went to the desk Williamson had been using and his phone. She touched the screen, but it required a four-digit password to see anything. If she were wrong about the phone number or Williamson, she'd feel like shit for doing this, but she was sure the number was the same—she had to check.

Sanchez was tech-savvy, but she was no codebreaker. Instead, she was pretty sure what a meathead like Williamson would use as his code. Hell, the fool had even made jokes about it in the past.

She typed in "5297." The screen lit up, displaying recent text notifications. The number on the most recent texts was from David's listed number.

Call me as soon as you can
Your gonna need a bigger boat
He's here now

The texts before those came from Barry Gillum.

Rory is there
Tomorrow at 12

A dozen thoughts flooded the chief's mind, but foremost was the fact that she had illegally searched her officer's phone, and that she had only a brief amount of time before someone came in. Sanchez pressed the correct pair of buttons on the phone to capture a screenshot of the texts, saved the image, and opened a new text screen. In the address bar, she typed in "c" and "h," and the phone filled in the "ief." She quickly sent herself a text with the screenshot messages, then deleted it from the list. She then went to the Photos tab, found the pics she had taken and sent, and then deleted them.

The chief put the phone down and headed back to her office when Williamson called on the radio that he (Sierra 1-2) was taking the Canadian to the ER and that Long (Papa 3-2) was going to bring Warren to the station. Sanchez grabbed the portable radio on her desk and chimed in, "Papa 3-2, Charlie 1."

"Go, Chief," Long replied.

"You take the subject to the ER. I'll have IST join you so you can get the records request started," the chief added to help give cover to her reasoning. "Have Sierra 3 bring the vic in here."

Long: "10-4! Out."

Sanchez readied herself. *This is gonna be interesting*, she thought. Within a minute, both Long and Williamson called dispatch to say they had cleared the scene and were en route to their respective destinations.

Within another minute, the back door of the squad room opened. The door had a passcode, and the officers could come and go without being buzzed in. Plus, it was less of a walk from the bar. The chief saw Williamson had a shitty look on his face, but neither acknowledged it. Warren walked in after the uniform and looked quite embarrassed.

"Hey, Chief!" he said without making eye contact.

Sanchez didn't respond. Instead, she told Williamson to do what he was already about to do. Take him to Interview Three and get a complete statement. Interview Three was an inside joke that had become part of Westwood PD's lexicon. They had one interview room. When they had more than one person to question, they'd have to take turns. It was called Three because it was the third door along that wall. Two was a supply closet, and Four was the chief's office.

"10-4," the cop said with an attitude that made the chief want to punch him square in his face right there and then.

Williamson had Warren sit in the interview room. "I'll be right back," he said to Warren. "You want some coffee or water?"

"Coffee, please. Cream and sugar," Warren replied politely.

He left the room, leaving the door open. Instead of going to the kitchen, Williamson turned left and headed back to the chief, who was still standing between her office door and the desk Williamson had been using.

"Why'd you switch me and Long?" Williamson asked sternly and with too much aggression. "I wanted to ask that Canuck a few things."

Her blood pressure rising, she held up her left index finger and pointed it at her cop. "One, because I fucking said so!" The chief knew she was overplaying her hand. She had to back off. "Two," she raised another finger to join the other, "we all know I know Warren from way back, so I wanna make certain that you give him plenty of shit during his final statement. Long knows we're friends, and he'd probably be too soft on him because of that. You? You do what you do best. Be a dick if you have to, but get the full story."

Williamson couldn't argue with that logic. He was a dick and enjoyed being tough with anyone who came under his control, whether they deserved it or not. The chief just gave him the green light to be tough on her buddy. He was probably going to like this.

Just then, Williamson's phone vibrated, and the chief used all her willpower not to look at it. Williamson did, though. He looked back at the chief and looked for any hint, any clue of extra knowledge.

"Okay, Chief," he said weakly. "I can do that."

He grabbed his phone and mug, turned, and headed to the kitchen for coffee.

"I already made another pot!" the chief added to Williamson's back. "Fucker!" she whispered.

When she saw her patrolman enter the kitchen, Sanchez hustled the few steps to the open door of the interview room and said quickly, "Roll with me on this one. Tell the truth, but also tell me every impression that you get about him when you're done. I'll tell you why later."

"What the f—" was all that Warren had time for before the chief left the doorway and headed back to her office.

35

"So …" the old cop started, "I know you're an old friend of the chief, and you've probably conducted a few of these yourself, so we're gonna make this all nice and friendly, okay? For the record, I'm Quinton Williamson, and I'd like to get a few more details about what happened at The Rathdrum Inn this evening."

Sanchez could see and hear the interview on the screen in her office. More importantly, she could see where Williamson was and if he had left that room. On her desk phone, she dialed Barry Gillum's cell number. She wasn't sure if he'd even answer, but she needed to shake the tree and see what might fall out. Even a voicemail would work, but Gillum picked up on the third ring.

"Hello?" His voice was hesitant.

"Barry Gillum?" Sanchez began. "This is Chief Sanchez with the Westwood Police. We chatted at your work yesterday."

"Sure, Chief." His voice was now hesitant and nervous. "What can I do for you?"

"I'd like to follow up on a few things regarding Mr. Baker. I was going to be out your way tomorrow afternoon, and I was hoping that I could swing by and chat. How about around twelve?"

The other end of the line was silent, but the chief could hear Gillum's tense breathing. "No, ma'am. I'm pretty sure that I'll be tied up tomorrow. Could we wait —"

"I don't get out that way much," the chief interrupted. "So even if you only have a few minutes, I'd appreciate it. If you're too busy for that, I'll still be there to drop off a copy of the updated warrant." There was no updated warrant. There's no such thing, but the chief was confident Gillum wouldn't know that.

Again, nothing but breathing from the other end of the line. She wasn't sure what was supposed to happen at twelve tomorrow or even where that "what" was supposed to occur, but Gillum's silence let her know it was probably at the mill.

"Oh! Just one more thing." Sanchez had let this line creep into her language over the years, but again was certain that Gillum was too young to catch the reference. "Before our visit yesterday, had you ever met Sergeant Williamson? He was the other officer that I was with."

Another long pause. She could almost hear the gears turning inside Gillum's head, trying to crank out a sensible answer. "No, ma'am. I don't believe so," he said quietly and with hesitancy.

"I just thought that since you both have been up here for so many years that your paths might have crossed." After a brief pause came one of her most trusted lines. "Are you sure?"

"Are you sure?" Such a simple question. Three little words. Over the past twenty-plus years of her career as a law enforcement professional, this simple question has been more helpful than almost any other. The answers she received may not always have been truthful, but there is a lot to learn from lies and how people tell them. Sure, it would have been better to ask him in person so she could read his face, but his tone told her as much in this case.

"…uh…no, ma'am," he sputtered. "I'm pretty sure that I'd never met him before."

It was her turn to be silent. She wasn't at a loss for words. She wanted his lie to hang in the air for another few moments.

"Okay, Mr. Gillum. Hopefully, I'll see you tomorrow. If not, I'll still swing by around noon. Have a good night." Sanchez spoke quickly and cut the call short. She enjoyed the idea of Gillum holding a dead phone to his ear while his head spun. Next, she settled into her desk chair and waited for a text or a call. She turned the volume back on so she could listen to Williamson and Warren.

Williamson: … were you out there?

Warren: Just exploring. I haven't been to that area, so I took some time to do so—lots of gravel roads and a few cool ponds.

Williamson: So you just drove around?

Warren: At a couple places, I got out to walk some trails that were out there. Hung out at a pond for a bit and watched a few ducks getting ready for the season.

Williamson: Kinda early and cold for ducks just yet, isn't it?

Warren: Tell that to the ducks. I took a few pics. Here! Let me show—

Williamson: Did anyone see you out there? Were you alone the whole time?

Warren: I can't say if anyone saw me, but I was alone as far as I could tell.

Williamson: Someone reported that a vehicle matching yours was parked along the highway near the mill entrance for an hour or so. Was that you?

Warren: Probably. I parked there and headed out for a walk along the tracks.

Williamson: See anything interesting?

On the screen, Sanchez could see Williamson reach into his pocket and grab his cell phone. He brought it close to his chest, concealing it from the camera he knew was behind him. That camera focused on the person in the other chair, but if one wasn't careful, what was displayed on the screen might show up in the video.

She saw his body freeze for a moment when he read the text. Williamson took a deep breath and continued with Warren.

Williamson: And from there, where did you go? Somewhere else, or is that when you came back to town?

Warren: I drove past my place on the way back here to see what was going on.

Williamson: Anything?

Warren: There was still a team out there doing their thing. I didn't stop. That's when I came back to the hotel.

She heard the phone vibrate this time because Williamson had set it on his chair between his legs. He looked at the message with no emotion or change in demeanor, but his questioning style shifted.

Williamson: Okay. You're at the bar. I've seen the video, but tell me one more time what happened.

The texts could have been from anyone, another cop, or some gal he's seeing, but the timing got the chief excited—and scared.

36

3 years earlier

For the next two hours, Warren sat in his cruiser, using his laptop to complete the paperwork required for any crime, large or small. The late-shift detectives and the crime scene team had arrived to do their thing while he kept an eye out for civilian foot or vehicle traffic that might come close, but none did.

By the time the CS techs finished their work and the coroner's team arrived to remove the body, his admin work was done, and the sun was rising in the east. Black cleared from the scene after the coroner's team left with the victim, and she added her report as a supplement to the larger file the detectives were compiling. Warren did the paperwork he needed for the murder book and could use the next shift, his last in a four-day run, to finish the rest.

On the way home, he stopped at his gym, needing the workout to help still his active mind. After a shower at home, sleep evaded him, and he lay in bed, planning how to handle the next step. That next step would be even more difficult: how to handle dirty money. Fortunately, Warren knew a guy, a guy who knew the ins and outs of finance law.

Though he got some light sleep, Warren spent the next thirty-six hours in a mix of tension and anxiety as he planned what to do. Some rest would come, then a long and tedious shift, followed by more restless sleep before he could act.

Warren parked his Honda on a small side street off Stadium Drive, about a quarter mile west of Stadium Diner. This street was as shabby and derelict as Bennington, but he was still careful to turn his lights off before he turned onto it. He parked on a gravel turnout next to two other abandoned cars and behind an old, wheelless flatbed trailer, where he killed his interior lights before opening his door and stepping out. He stood silently, listening to the light wind around him and the traffic from the nearby freeways—nothing out of the ordinary or close by. The southern end of the block held a home that might be occupied, but there weren't any lights on and no activity, so it didn't give cause for concern. Wearing an oversized hoodie and slightly baggy jeans, Warren adopted a walk that was far more casual than the crisp, military stride with which he normally moved and headed south along the street, and made a left at the end of it. From his patrols in the area, he knew the street was a dead end. It had a small trail at its end that led through the woods to Leeds Trafficway, a busy road during work hours but another dead zone this time of the morning. From Leeds, he walked east, found the small trail along the Blue River, and followed it to Stadium Drive and the bridge that crossed it.

He could see the diner lights a few blocks up and wanted to avoid any possible eyes. After he crossed, he quickly found the trail along the east bank of the Blue River. He followed it until he reached the footpath that led from the river to 39th Street. The street was black except for a circle of light near the gated entrance of the old truck depot halfway down the block. Warren wasn't sure if the depot was still in use, but he had never seen any signs of activity or occupants. Still, though, he skirted the light as best he could and continued to Bennington Street. Just as it had been two nights prior, it was dead quiet. No sound. No lights. No movement.

He stayed on the west side of the street to hide in the shadows cast by the giant beech tree near the abandoned house on the corner. He moved across to the other side as he approached the old business buildings, hiding in doorways if needed, using the shadows beneath the awnings that still hung in front.

Slowing as he neared his target shop, he scoured the ground to see if any disturbances in the dirt, gravel, or dust might indicate other foot traffic. None. He moved slowly, passed the door he wanted, and made it to the end of the building, where he paused. In the shadow of the doorway of the first shop, Warren gave another look and listened—still nothing. A block to the west, the diner was empty. He returned to his shop and repeated his actions from the other night: prying off the board, setting it aside, and quickly stepping through the frame. He looked for any fresh disturbances in the debris on the floor but found none. Finding the chair where he had left it, he grabbed it, placed it under the open ceiling tile, and climbed up. The old insulation, too, was where he had left it, unmolested. With a quick pull, it was out of his way, and the leather case was staring him down, daring him to complete his crime. He did.

Stepping down from the chair, he placed it back where he found it, then swept the floor with his foot to erase any marks he had created. He returned to the window frame, checked the surroundings, stepped through, placed the case on the ground, and grabbed the board. The flashlight again worked perfectly as a hammer, and as soon as it was in place over the opening, Warren turned to scan the area. Nothing.

On foot, he retraced the same route through the neighborhood, along the river, across the bridge, and back to his car without seeing a soul. A car passed on a nearby street, but he never saw it; he only heard its engine. He entered his Honda, started it without the headlights, drove down the road and onto E 35th Terrace in the dark, and turned on his lights only when he crested the hill and headed back toward the parkway.

For a moment, the freedom of being in the broader street and in the bright lights gave him a feeling of escape, like he had passed the worst of the risks. Whether he had or hadn't, Warren couldn't relax yet. He still had to process the case, but everything was in place for that.

Warren pulled into the driveway of the storage area he had rented and prepared the day before. It was a shady place, and its manager didn't ask any questions when he paid six months in advance. The 10'x14' space was secure and had electrical outlets. That's all he needed. He parked his car an aisle away from his unit and, before leaving the vehicle, placed the leather case inside a large plastic shopping bag. The odds of anyone ever seeing Warren, his car, or the case were already slim. Still, every action he took minimized the chance that anyone would see him or recall anything suspicious.

Removing the two padlocks, he opened the rolling door a few feet, slid inside, and shut the door behind him. In the dark, Warren reached for the electrical cord he had set up. He flicked the switch on it, and the lights he had brought in came to life. He secured one of the padlocks to the rail of the sliding door so that it couldn't be opened from the outside.

The "processing station" was prepared and waiting for him. Warren had little clue where this money had been, whose it was, or what precautions had been taken. Just by the fact that it was still in the place that he put it on the night of the murder, he was certain that it didn't have a transponder or tracking chip, but was less sure of whether it had a dye pack, and he wanted to be sure. So here, he had a hazmat room within the room, essentially, with plastic Visqueen on the ceilings, floors, and four walls. It was about six feet by six feet, but that space, the lights, his biosuit, and the small table he had set up were all he would need.

Warren opened the clasp of the bag he had set in the center of the table and took out the first bundle, $20s. He picked it up, examined it through the plastic visor on his suit's headpiece, and set it aside. The plan was to remove one bundle at a time, examine it carefully, and sort it into two piles: one for $20s with violet straps and another for $100s with mustard-colored bands. The piles were shielded by more plastic. If a dye pack did explode, at least some of the cash could be salvaged.

Since the night that he first grabbed the case, he had jostled and tossed it around enough that if it were to have a dye pack, it probably would have gone off already. All the bundles of bills in the case would be marked with a distinct indigo color, and the bills would be rendered useless. Anyone who saw them would know to contact the police or the Feds. So far—nothing.

More bundles, still no explosions of blue. The two piles grew, with the $100s quickly outpacing the $20s. With the contents of the bag exhausted, Warren couldn't help but feel a little silly for his abundance of caution. The odds of the case being tracked or rigged were slim to begin with, but the idea of going to work the next day covered in blue ink was enough to make him tread wisely. It turned out to be a waste of time, but the actions put him at ease.

That's a lot of money! Warren thought to himself. Before he could get too far ahead on this track, he got back to work. He stepped out of his square plastic bubble and took off his biosuit. He grabbed the plastic shopping bag, went back into the tent, and packed the bundles into it. He tore down the plastic walls and ceiling, then stuffed them into a black trash bag he had brought. He set the table next to the door and picked up the plastic on the floor.

Within a minute, he had everything bagged and near the door, save the lights and the two electrical cords. He removed the padlock from the rail, grabbed his gym bag and the white trash bag containing the cash bundles, turned off the lights, and headed out. He didn't worry about securing the door yet, merely closing it before heading to his car.

Warren pulled up to his unit and spent less than ninety seconds loading the remaining items into the back of his Honda. Sweeping with his flashlight, he made sure to leave nothing inside the unit. He re-secured the padlocks and left, never to return. In six months, he would call the manager and tell him he was done and that he could cut the padlocks off. He used false information in the rental and knew the place had no video cameras. His connection here was done.

On his drive home, he stopped at a dumpster in a nearby business park to discard the plastic sheeting and biosuit. Because this was in his patrol area and he had a police radio, he knew the dumpster would be picked up later that morning and that no patrol units were nearby.

Karl Warren headed home flush with clean cash and several heavyweight questions: How much was in the bag? Whose money is it? Why was this guy murdered? Why didn't they know about the money? Who will be looking for it?

And the most critical question: now what?

37

As the interview was wrapping up, she turned off the room's video feed. Williamson came out alone, stepped into her office, and said, "We're all done. He's clear. You need anything from him?"

"No," she said. "Kick him loose and tell him I'll call him tomorrow with an update.

She heard Williamson say his goodbyes and share the chief's message before he escorted Warren out the front door. He didn't step into the chief's office when he came back. Instead, he returned to his desk and began typing up the paperwork for the interview and the case. At their respective desks, they worked silently, but Sanchez saw Williamson on his phone, texting someone. Gillum, she assumed.

She was also texting.

Are you back at the hotel?

Warren's text came back saying that he was.

**Stay there. We need to
chat. Be there in 30.**

The chief dove back into her work. Williamson was doing the same. He had put his phone down and hadn't looked at it for a while. Whatever important information needed to be shared had been shared so that the old cop could pay full attention to his admin chores.

After killing another twenty minutes shuffling papers and pretending to work, Sanchez logged off her terminal and secured the files she had been using. She yelled out, "I'm done. What's your status?"

"Almost finished. Long is still at KMC, but he's logged on and getting his report done. If he finishes before I'm off, I'll add it to the book."

"Excellent!" she said with false cheer. There was no way Long could add anything beyond the Canadian's initial statement. The rest would take a couple of days. "Whatever you get done, make sure you're available until Husted comes on. I'll see you after your weekend."

Adrian Husted was the newest officer on the team and, thus, had been working graveyards since he finished his field training. He started riding solo just as winter weather began and, over the following six months, became an expert at driving through the worst the Inland Northwest could muster. He'd begin his ten-hour shift at 10 pm and stay long enough to provide overlap for the two officers who started at 7 am.

Sanchez grabbed her personal gear and headed out the back door to the lot where her vehicle sat, next to the department's Ford Explorer, hers and hers alone to use. She could use it off duty if she wanted, but she liked the idea of some separation between work and personal life in this small town.

She drove down Main Street past the Rathdrum and parked around the corner. Still in uniform, she headed inside. Warren was in his spot on the far side of the bar counter. She said hello to Murphy and the two townies who were at the bar watching Family Feud on the screen above the mirror. "Howdy, Chief!" Murphy said warmly. "Get you a beer?"

"Not tonight, or at least not yet. How about a Diet Coke, though?" she said back to him with equal warmth. Murphy Longman was one of the first folks in town she met when she got the job, and the many lunches at the convenient spot gave them more opportunities to get to know each other better.

Warren saw her as soon as she entered. He nodded and waited for her to get her drink and come over. She didn't. Instead, after getting her Diet Coke, she motioned with her head that they should move to one of the booths near the back. Warren collected his drink but left his cash. He planned to be back for more.

Sanchez stayed silent and appeared tense. Warren broke the ice first. "So. What's up?" The chief looked as if she were about to speak, but said nothing. Instead, she shifted in her seat, trying to find where to start. Years of writing reports, testifying in courts, and instructing at the KCPD Academy taught her all she needed to know about conveying information.

But she began with a question: "What did you think of Williamson during your chat?"

"He strikes me as being badge-heavy," Warren said. "He enjoys the power of controlling people. Despite that, he was methodical in his questions, asking the same thing in a few different ways to cross-check. I thought that maybe he was being tense or adversarial to get more out of me, but—but I think he's just an asshole. He lost his rhythm when he got some texts, but he got back in form soon enough. Was that you who texted him?"

"No," she said. "Not me."

"Who then?"

She paused, both for dramatic effect and to make sure she wanted to share all this with him.

"Barry Gillum," she finally said.

"Well, that is unexpected!" Warren said. He leaned forward to be closer to her words. He spoke them as if to conserve their energy as they flew from his mouth to her ears.

The chief put both of her elbows on the table and leaned over it. "Here's what we have so far. Forgive me if I say something you already know," she started. "We have dead bodies at your place, formerly Charles Baker's place. He used to work at the mill. Gillum has his position now. Apparently, they were tight back in the day. Goodson had the files, but a month was missing. When I went to your place today to check on the progress, my guys had found a bunch of Baker's old papers and keepsakes—including that missing month. Your girls are fine, by the way. I collected a few eggs and put them in your fridge."

Warren thought for a moment and seemed to let the new information slip into place. He may have known or assumed a few of these things, but the missing pieces probably made for a clearer image. Sanchez was sure that knowing that his girls were doing well was an immense relief, too.

"So, Goodson has blackmail info with all the fake and real copies of the EPA paperwork. That paperwork showed what the real discharge levels were from the mill, levels that the EPA would probably close the mine down for. Or maybe fine them into bankruptcy. Gillum was married then but divorced now, so there's no reason to deny knowing her unless he had something to do with her disappearance. Baker was "The Fixer" out there, so maybe he fixed this problem. Perhaps he got wind of Goodson's plan and killed her. He thought he had all her files, so there was no need to look for more."

"Yeah," the chief interjected, "that might make sense, but what about the other girls? Had Baker been doing this for a while before her, or did he get a taste of it and make it a hobby afterward?"

"A lot will depend on the IDs of the bodies and setting a timeline of their disappearances. Wait!" Warren paused. "What does Williamson have to do with this?"

"Ah!" she said as she got back on track. "While Williamson was here dealing with you, he left his phone at the station. I may or may not have completely violated his rights by illegally accessing his device." She told Warren she had recognized the phone numbers in the most recent texts, then seen the ones from Gillum.

Warren had to chew this one over. "So ... Williamson is working with Gillum? What's going on at twelve tomorrow?"

"While Williamson was interviewing you, I called Gillum to shake the tree. I told him I'd be out there around noon tomorrow to talk to him again. He seemed to dislike that idea not a single bit. He tried to get out of it, but I pressed on. I'm assuming the texts that Will got when he was with you were from Gillum." The chief paused again to collect her thoughts. After a full minute of silence, she continued, "So ... what's happening at twelve tomorrow?"

38

The chief had left, but not before she and I settled on a tentative plan. She'd start the day with the city attorney to clarify the legal path regarding Williamson's employment rights. At the very least, she wanted to suspend him. Still, she wasn't even sure she could do that, since she'd gathered her evidence about Williamson illegally. Then she'd call Captain Petrelli at IST to pick his brain about the path forward for a criminal investigation into both Williamson and anyone at the mill who might have known about the Goodson blackmail and her disappearance. Again, she had the problem of the illegally discovered texts, but at least she had the missing inspection files and the items from my, rather, Baker's barn.

I was back on my original perch with another Jack and Coke. The plan of attack we had come up with had nothing for me to do, so I was left with another night of drinking and Netflix. The calm I'd been showing since the fight earlier was fake. I knew I needed to present a cool outer shell to sell the idea of my innocence in the matter. I honestly was a "victim" in this case, but habits are habits. Inside, though, my mind was whirling. Adrenaline doesn't go back into its bottle as quickly as it comes out, and it often takes me a couple of hours for my heart rate and breathing to return to normal. When they do, there's still a restlessness and hyper-alertness that linger even longer. Next would come the depression, but I wasn't there yet. I needed to move.

Leaving a buck per drink, I gathered my remaining cash and told Murphy that I was gonna head out for a walk.

"That's fine!" Murphy said. 'I may close at midnight, so if you come after that, use the door at the end of the storefront. Your room key will open it, and you can head upstairs from there."

State Highway 53 carved off a piece of Westwood and, along with the railroad tracks that ran alongside it, left a residential neighborhood physically separated from the rest of the town. A few small businesses existed along the highway. Most importantly, it had another bar, The Deadhead. I could have spent time walking around the older parts of town to see the wonderful old Victorian homes a block away from downtown, but I wasn't in the mood to play tourist. I was in the mood to drink.

The railroad tracks ran through a tunnel, allowing safe passage for pedestrians and cyclists from the town proper to the other side of the highway. There was a pedestrian crossing, but it was still a risky walk during busy times. A fully loaded timber or gravel truck would have a hard time stopping for anyone who jumped onto that crosswalk, assuming they had some magic shield of safety.

At night, though, the only danger for me was the siren song of the neon sign at the bar. I'd had enough walking. Enough thinking. With its bouts of heavy mist and intermittent rainfall, the cool night air had dampened my buzz, and the bad thoughts were coming back: bodies in my soil, and what might have happened to them. It was time for self-medication.

The Deadhead was a fire waiting to happen. The pothole-filled parking lot may have been safe from flames, but starting with several years' worth of dead weeds and grass in the flower beds and going up to the old cedar shake roof, everything in between was way past its expiration date. The fir board-and-batten siding looked as if it had been painted red when the first pioneers came here. The windows may have been cleaned at the same time.

Details like that didn't seem to matter much as the crowd here, though still modest, was bigger than anything I'd seen at The Rathdrum. The northbound lane of Highway 53 had an extensive shoulder, and three big rigs sat parked out there. Were they getting their federally mandated rest periods, or were they inside getting their drink on before they went further north into the dark?

The inside would have seemed cozy except for the haze of cigarette smoke. Idaho law still allowed smoking in bars. Murphy didn't allow it in his place, much to my delight, but that may also explain why he had fewer patrons than he might. Of the twelve people inside this bar, most were smoking up a storm, and I almost turned around to leave when I saw someone at the back table staring at me. Williamson. Like any cop, he had chosen a seat that would let him see the whole place and who might be entering.

I froze for a moment and had to make a quick decision. The sensible thing would be to back out and call it a night. There was no need to stir the pot. I saw Williamson with someone, but I couldn't tell who.

Leaving was the right choice. I went to the bar and ordered a Jack and Coke.

The bartender was another mountain of a man, a younger version of Murphy Longman, but with a shaved head and goatee, wearing denim and leather. More biker than logger. He approached warily without saying a word. He smelled of cigarettes and dirty rags. I ordered a drink and set a $20 bill on the bar top. The bartender wordlessly set the drink down, took the bill, and returned the change. Though recently wiped, the bar was still sticky, like a toddler had run their drool-crusted hands across it.

"Thanks," I said to him. The big man stood in front of me, sizing me up.

"You're the cop, huh?" he said it as a slur. "The chicken rancher," he added with a smile.

39

Gillum saw Williamson's eyes light up when he looked at the door. After a moment, he looked over to see a man walk from the entrance to the bar. "Who's that?" he asked.

"That's Warren," the old cop told him.

"What the fuck is he doing here? Did he follow one of us? Did you tell him we were meeting?" Gillum's voice wavered, and his eyes darted around the room.

"Calm the fuck down!" Williamson said in a hushed but inarguable tone. "Shut up for a minute!"

Williamson needed time to consider what this might mean. If Gillum didn't know Warren, maybe Warren didn't know him. Or, more likely, the chief told him about the documents she found and the Gillum connection. He still didn't know if the chief's meeting tomorrow was coincidental or if she somehow knew that the money exchange would happen. He was also pretty sure his connection to this mess was still unknown. Gillum was already the weak link, and now, with Warren showing up here, that relationship was even more confusing and problematic. Had he followed Gillum or him?

Williamson turned his attention back to Gillum. "Who else did you tell about the chief's call?"

"Just you and Mallard," Gillum said. "I called him before I texted you. Should we postpone the transfer tomorrow?"

"No," said Williamson. "There's no way to do that. The only excuse good enough to cancel would be to tell them the truth about this heat. If we did that, not only would we not get paid, they'd never do business with us again. We'd be stuck with all the product and a pissed-off Ukrainian family. So, no!"

"What about Warren? Why the fuck is he here?" It was more of a statement of frustration than a question from Gillum. "We gotta move the transfer back a couple days. We don't even have to tell them why."

Williamson went quiet again, doing some mental gymnastics. He knew the slightest bump here could spell doom. As far as he knew, Warren, in seeing this meeting, knew the sole link between him and the mill, and he was equally sure neither Warren nor Sanchez knew about the drug shipments. They had done nothing wrong. The problem began when Warren found Baker's old kills, and the chief started sniffing into Baker's past at the mill. Gillum fucked all that up by lying to the chief about his history with his girl. Had he played it cool, she might not have felt the need to visit her mother's house.

Now, Gillum getting spooked and needing to be held by the hand led to a new potential problem: Warren seeing them together. He was certain he could explain that away if he had to. That would leave a trail. The problem was Gillum, and he feared he would have to handle it himself.

"Get out of here. Go home," he said to Gillum. "Just go home and call in sick tomorrow. I'll take care of it with Mallard. You stay home and don't say a fucking word to anyone.

"But they'll need me at the mill tomorrow!" he said.

"No," he spat back. "They don't need you at the mill tomorrow. It's a load transfer like any other. It's a product shuffle and an extra suitcase. Mallard and I can handle it. Go the fuck home. Keep your head down and keep your fucking mouth shut. I'll call you tomorrow with any news. Now get out of here."

Gillum looked both stunned and hurt, as if his father had told him they wouldn't be getting a puppy because of his poor grades. He remained silent as he slid out of his chair, headed toward the back door, and faded into the night.

At the moment, Warren's presence was the biggest problem. He had to get out of there without causing a conflict or starting a conversation. And he had to do it before Warren left. If Warren went before him, he'd be worried that the chicken farmer would follow Gillum. He had to get out soon, ahead of the ex-cop. His tab was paid up, so he wouldn't have to spend time on that. He just had to leave.

He got out of his chair and headed toward the front door. There was no way to avoid Warren's sight, so as he passed, he made eye contact, gave a polite nod and smile, and headed on. Williamson saw Warren return the nod and raise his glass before he hit the panic bar on the door to escape.

The moment he stepped outside, he called Mallard.

"Gillum is freaked out," Williamson said into the phone. His speech was rushed but still calm. "He wants to postpone the transfer because he's worried about the chief's visit tomorrow."

"That would be stupid," said Mallard. "We'd piss off both north and south. We can't do that because Gillum's scared."

A heavy silence settled on the conversation for a few seconds.

Mallard broke the silence. "Do it! Get rid of him. I'll clean things up at work in case the chief visits."

"Will do," the old cop said. "I'll see you tomorrow." He ended the call.

The last time Williamson straight-up murdered someone, he didn't have to worry about hiding the body. This time, he'd have to use some lessons learned from Cha, who, as it turns out, was the last person he had killed.

40

I didn't stay long at The Deadhead. Besides the fact that I was conspicuous as hell, the place had way too many flickering neon lights, pinging pinball games, and motion all around. Plus, the bar smelled like a wet rag, and it was all I could do not to let it taint my Jack and Coke. It was probably too late to grab a drink at The Rathdrum, so I asked the bald, ashtray-scented mountain behind the bar if I could grab something to go. He said no, but in a way that made me think it would be a yes for anyone else. It was time to get out of here.

The drizzle had returned but was barely more than a heavy mist. Refreshing, actually. Its wetness provided a safe envelope in which to gather my thoughts. All sound and movement in the town were muffled, and it made me feel safe. I needed that after today. I needed it to make sense of what had happened. Calling the chief was an option, but it was too late at night. We'll catch up tomorrow. We had the noon meeting at the mill to discuss how we would handle it.

By the time I got to my room, I realized I was exhausted and glad I hadn't gotten the extra beer. At the same time, the additional alcohol would have helped make me feel better about the shithole that I had landed in. As I lay in bed, my mind jumped through hoops trying to get a sense of how Williamson fit into this, and I saw a picture I didn't like. If Williamson knew Gillum, did he know Baker? If so, how much of Baker's activities did he know about? What does Williamson have to do with the deliveries at the mill, if anything? Nothing was clear yet, other than that the town was dirty and damaged in a way I hadn't expected.

Perhaps it was all the rain that made me choose a nature documentary about the oceans and whales. I vaguely recall Sir David Attenborough describing how humpback whales would gather in small teams, forming circles and blowing bubbles as they rose from the depths. This action corralled the thousands of herring together, and the whales from the pod could open their mouths wide as they surfaced and swallowed countless fish all at once. Magnificent to watch in high definition if you're a fan of whales, but terrifying if you're a tiny herring being wrangled by tremendous forces into the gullet of a creature beyond your comprehension.

As if that wasn't bad enough for the herring, being that they were all near the surface now because of the wall of bubbles made by the whales, even if you were lucky enough to escape the maw of the cetaceans, you had scores of gulls and other birds waiting to swoop in and grab a fish that came too close to the surface. Life was tough all around.

Whales and gulls need the herring. The herring eat other smaller creatures. The chickens eat mice and grain. The mice eat grain, too. Everything needs something to live, but Cha, Cha didn't need to do what he did to survive. The whales weren't evil. The coyotes that wanted my chickens weren't evil. Cha was evil.

I knew that sleep would come soon tonight, and I hoped the ghosts wouldn't come with it. They may or may not be evil ones; I just didn't like their visits.

41 - Saturday

Upon return to his home on the hillside, Williamson, though tired from the long day, went straight into action. He was nervous about what lay ahead, but oddly excited, too. In his spare time, he'd often thought about how he'd dispose of a dead body, and now he had the chance to put that plan into play.

Most of what he'd need was already in the back of his truck: kerosene, a small mallet, a cutting maul, and small-gauge hemp rope. To this, he added a canvas drop cloth, two small garbage bags, and his battery-powered leaf blower. Last, he threw in some kindling and well-aged tamarack splits left over from the winter's firewood.

This still left him with some time to kill. The plan was to leave his home around 2 am and head toward Gillum's place. By then, the bars would be closed, and all their patrons and staff would be home and off the road. A random traveler may be on the state highway, but Gillum's neighborhood would be empty. The wildcard would be the graveyard patrol, Husted. *The rookie is stupid enough to be dangerous*, he thought. Williamson had a police scanner to keep an ear out for where he might be, so he felt confident the young cop wouldn't be a problem. He set his phone's alarm to sound off at 1:30 and lay in his well-worn recliner to catch a few minutes of sleep.

If the next day goes smoothly, he thought, *I'll be a whole new person soon. Gonna have to lie low in*

Montana for a while, but may end up in Canada. The cause has plenty of brothers in Alberta and Saskatchewan. I'll have to get back into the trades or maybe logging again, but I'll have plenty of cash and plenty of space to roam.

Initially, as a younger man, he had started in logging and trucking, but thought better of it. Not that he was afraid of hard work. It's that he wanted a better, safer, warmer way to spend the long winters. He saw the other men in his clan dying or becoming hobbled in accidents or getting ground down to nubs as the hard work took its toll over the years. His now-dead family had a friend on the Westwood city council. That and his associate's degree from North Idaho College were all it took to get a slot on the Westwood PD.

While a police officer, he let his blue-collar background, personal grudge, and family's sociopolitical grooming take hold. He showed this in how he enforced the laws he liked and on whom he enforced them. You're a local logger with a domestic violence problem? As long as Quint comes to your call, you'll be okay unless your spouse is seriously injured. You're a young kid from Spokane passing through town with a joint in your car? Plan on having a very bad day in Westwood. You're a fellow cop who got caught with a seventeen-year-old high school girl? Quint will have your back and talk to the parents about how damaging this would be to the young girl's reputation in such a small town. You're a visiting Canadian tourist down to buy cheap cigarettes from Walmart in Post Falls? Don't pass through Westwood if your car's lights aren't fully working, or you'll experience every possible fine from the City of Westwood and the State of Idaho.

One fine summer day, when Williamson was in his fourth year as an officer and feeling in a good groove, he pulled over a classic Dodge Charger. Though he personally admired the red-and-black machine, it had Montana plates and was therefore a fair target. The car was speeding into town on Highway 53 from Washington, and even though it slowed to the legal limit as it neared town, the damage had been done, and Williamson had the speed locked on the radar gun's readout.

"You're Alton's boy, ain't you?" The man in the driver's seat said, after spying the nameplate, his own badge hanging from his wallet, leaning against the frame of the open window. The badge was from Lewis and Clark County in west-central Montana, and the man holding it looked like someone from west-central Montana should. "Sorry about the speeding coming into town. You mind lettin' me go with a cussin' out?"

"That depends," Williamson said. "How do you know my old man?"

"Hell!" the older deputy said. "Your old man and mine used to cause trouble back in their day. Back when our folks were truckers."

"Well, I bet you've got some embarrassing stories about him that I'd like to hear sometime. What were you doing in Idaho today?"

"Oh, I was just visiting some compatriots of ours," the old deputy said.

"Ours?" Williamson said, more bemused than surprised.

"Yeah, ours," Montana said again. "We're a bunch of cops and vets that get together and try to affect change through social and political pressure. You can call us a civil rights organization, of a sort," he said that part with a wry smile.

"We're all upset with how soft our society has turned and how lenient law enforcement has become. At the same time, government is, as always, sticking its nose where it doesn't belong. I'm not talkin' about this stop." He gave a gentle laugh. "You got me dead to rights here. No doubt I was coming into town too fast, and I'll take my lumps if I have to. Instead, though, let me go with that cussin' out, we'll exchange cards, and you'll already have a friend inside the group."

Williamson appreciated the boldness of the offer, but it was more than that. The idea of the group struck a chord with him. He'd been on the force a few years and could see how many rights the criminals had, how easy he had to go on the illegals, and how many hoops he had to jump through to get permission to get anything done. Hell, the out-of-state wolf lovers had more say here than the local elk hunters about handling wildlife issues.

This new alliance probably wouldn't lead anywhere, but it was an intriguing idea. Plus, there's no harm in letting a brother cop off with a minor speeding ticket, so after exchanging business cards and a friendly "cussin' out," Williamson returned to his patrol car. A new idea had taken root in his mind, one that would eventually develop into his escape from his current predicament.

42

Chimes. Delicate, little chimes. That was the sound that Williamson used for his alarm. He woke easily but remained still for a moment to let his blood rush and his thoughts focus. He'd become such a light sleeper in the past few years that it took only the slightest sound to wake him. With so few neighbors within a mile, their noise rarely reached him, but more than once, the coyotes that roamed near his land would wake him with their yipping. During the right time of year, he could hear male elk bugling.

After a few moments, he gathered the last tools he needed. From his nightstand, he retrieved his personal sidearm, a Glock 23. From a box tucked away in his closet, he grabbed a stun gun, a Ruger .22, and the homemade silencer that came with it. He had found a load of great tools and toys at crime scenes and during traffic stops over the years and had availed himself of many of the more enticing pieces. These were finally going to be put to good use. Last, he took a banana to eat along the way. He could feel his blood sugar was off and didn't want it to distract him while taking care of Gillum. Keys in hand, he headed out to his truck, started it up, and drove down the road.

Gillum lived in a small house, more of a cottage, really, two blocks from The Deadhead. The place had been his parents' home before him, but it was all his now that his father had passed away and his mother had retired and moved south. What had once been a modest and sensible home with a lovely garden had, over the years of young Gillum's custodianship, turned into yet another pile of weeds, scrap lumber, and dead motorcycle parts in the neighborhood. Few of the neighbors cared, but they missed the rose bushes Mrs. Gillum had invested so much effort in.

Except for the glow of the two streetlights down the block at Westwood City Park, the streets and intersections in this part of town were dark. Williamson killed his truck's lights before turning onto Gillum's street and let the remaining ambient light guide him to a space near the house, where an overgrowth of ninebark and hawthorn would conceal it from any errant eyes that might be up and about at this hour. He knew many people in this area got up early for long commutes to mills up north or to jobs in Spokane, so he had to be quick.

He'd been to Gillum's home a few times, and he knew the layout well. There were no lights inside the house, but he moved cautiously in case a motion-sensor light was on the back porch. He assumed not, but prepared for it anyway. Nothing. As he approached, Williamson was pleased that the decking looked new and that whoever built it had used tough, pressure-treated lumber. That meant fewer squeaks to worry about.

He knew Gillum never locked his door, but he was still relieved when the handle turned easily, and the door cracked open. The fine citizens of Westwood trusted their police force to keep them safe, so few locked their doors. Opening it a little wider, he stepped one foot inside and leaned forward to listen. Nothing other than light snoring from the bedroom.

He moved ahead smoothly and quickly, suppressed pistol in his hand. Reaching the open door of the bedroom, he moved his flashlight with its red lens cover around the room to ensure that no one else was there, then put his gun away.

"Hey, Barry," he said in a firm yet gentle tone. No response. "Gillum," he said it louder and sharper. This got a mumble and a slight stir from the sleeping man.

"Gillum! Get up! We have to get to the mill!" Williamson said, hoping that he wouldn't have to explain too much.

"Quint?" Gillum said. "Is that you? What are you—"

"We have to go, kid. Big problem with the transfer, but we can fix it easily."

"What? What problem?" Gillum said.

"I'll tell you on the way. Get dressed and grab your stuff," he said, leaving no room for argument.

Williamson told him he didn't want any neighbors to know he was here, so there would be no lights on as they left. Gillum got ready but did so with the reluctant air of an eight-year-old being forced to attend church. He put on the same clothes he had thrown on the floor when he came home from the bar, grabbed his keys and phone, and said, "Okay. Let's go!"

They went out the back door and headed to the truck along the same path Williamson had taken to the house. Wordlessly, they slipped into the truck. As soon as he got settled in the passenger seat and Williamson turned on the engine, Gillum rolled the window down and lit a cigarette. Williamson didn't smoke but didn't mind Gillum doing so if the windows were open. Instead, he reached into the inside pocket of his Carhartt coat, pulled out the silenced pistol without Gillum seeing it, and placed it between his legs.

With his lights still off, Williamson drove forward from where he had parked and entered the residential street again. He took a right at the next intersection and crept through it, keeping his eyes and ears open for anyone who might have seen them. With one more left turn, they were on McCartney Street, which led to Highway 53. Half a block from the highway, Williamson turned on his lights, rolled to a stop at the stop sign, and looked both ways before making his turn—and his eyes locked on Officer Adrian Husted across the roadway.

* * *

Husted had parked his cruiser at the gas station two blocks to the north and had been on a foot patrol of the few businesses along the highway. That done, he crossed the road to eyeball the few big rigs parked on the broad shoulder. He hadn't planned on rousting any of them, but if something seemed amiss—unsafe trailers or bad registration—he would call the troopers and have them pull the truck over later.

Just as he approached the tail end of the last semi on the shoulder, the headlights of a truck coming out of the neighborhood caught his eye. He recognized the truck and driver right away. Sergeant Williamson.

Damn, Husted thought. He both respected and feared the older cop. Husted knew he should have called dispatch to say he was on foot and hoped Williamson didn't have a radio. They had made eye contact, but the truck hadn't moved. Maybe Williamson wanted me to come over, Husted thought. Better to get this over with.

* * *

Williamson's whole body froze as his mind raced. Across the road, Husted smiled, waved, and walked over to say hello. The old cop had about fifteen seconds to think and concoct a story. He knew that being seen, not once but twice, with Gillum the day before he disappeared, would be disastrous for his plan. There was no way out except through it.

Husted came toward the truck and said, "Hey, Will! What are you doing up so— " His words cut short when the first of the three bullets entered his face.

In the passenger seat, Gillum was stunned and frozen, making no sound. Williamson switched the pistol from his right hand to his left, swung it around, and raised it to Gillum's face. Though it may be completely natural to use your hands to protect oneself from danger, the gesture proved utterly useless as two bullets went through Gillum's hands and into his head.

"Fuck," the old cop said calmly. He took two deep cleansing breaths to give himself time to think. This hurt his plans but didn't ruin them entirely. He'd just have to take a few extra steps. Time was valuable here.

He dropped his pistol on the dashboard and stepped out of the truck. He turned back to look inside and retrieve the five shells that he had shot. Finding them and stuffing them in his pocket, he turned to Husted. The young man had fallen in place, as if someone had flipped his off switch. The .22 rounds weren't powerful enough to blow him back with much force, and the wounds were minor and relatively bloodless. A few drops of dark, shiny crimson showed on the asphalt.

When not doing police work, Williamson spent much of his time hauling logs and doing farmwork, so hoisting a skinny kid like Husted wasn't much work. Tossing him in the truck bed, Williamson grabbed the canvas drop cloth and covered the dead cop with it. He weighed it down with some firewood, but not before grabbing Husted's radio and one of the trash bags. In the truck's cab, he leaned Gillum's body forward and slipped the bag over his bloody head. There was already a mess in the cab, but Williamson hoped this would prevent more blood and gore from soiling his truck.

He couldn't do anything about the police cruiser, so he had to leave it. There were a few drops of blood on the driver's door of the truck, but not enough to be overly noticeable. There wasn't time to clean it up anyway. He was in a vulnerable position and could be spotted at any moment. He had to leave. Stepping back out of the cab, he took one more quick circuit around it, looked around the area for witnesses, and got back in.

Less than three minutes after stopping at the stop sign, Williamson turned left onto the highway and headed northeast.

43

5 years earlier

Cha Baker still hunted deer and elk, albeit more slowly and in less remote areas than in his prime. Williamson knew Baker favored a desolate spot on paper company land west of Spirit Lake and knew the morning he'd be going. With that info, it was straightforward planning; he headed out before the old man made it to the last, curvy stretch of one-lane back road and waited for him.

Once parked, he could see Baker's truck coming. Williamson pulled out of the small turnoff where he had been sitting and blocked the road entirely with his vehicle. He gave a quick wave to put the man at ease and stepped out onto the roadway. He saw Baker relax the moment he recognized him and his truck. Good. He approached the driver's window as it lowered and said a quick hello.

"What the fuck are you doing out here?" the old man said, but as the words left his mouth, they softened as he figured it out himself.

In his retirement, Baker was getting too comfortable and talkative. On more than one occasion, word got to Williamson that Baker, usually over drinks, would drop a word or two about some past sin, either of the mill's or of his alone, that a casual listener might not pick up on. Still, anyone who had been associated with him in his days of dirty work with bribes, fraud, and murder would know precisely what he meant. Mallard

217

said it was best for the man to go away, and Williamson didn't disagree. There was too much at stake.

Silence hung in the air like the low clouds that sat on the mountains, covering up the ridges but low enough to let the tops peek through. The sound of the truck's old but powerful engine disturbed the natural world. Williamson offered a sad half-smile before quickly withdrawing a stun gun from his left pocket and forcing it onto Baker's exposed throat. A few seconds of contact, and it was done. He replaced the stun gun where it had come from and opened the driver's door, moving first across the stunned man to unbuckle his seatbelt.

The next part was going to be tricky. Williamson looked around to find a stick or branch that was about three feet long. Finding a perfect one, he returned to the open door and, with his left hand, used the stick to depress the brake pedal. Satisfied it was firmly planted, he reached in with his free hand, moved the steering-wheel-mounted gearshift from P to D, and took an additional step back. He switched the stick to his right hand, keeping the pressure on the pedal. Next, he turned the steering wheel hard to the right with his now-free left hand. He'd have to move quickly to stay out of the way, but once he was sure of his footing, he promptly withdrew the stick from the brake pedal and watched engineering and gravity take care of the rest.

Once he released the brake, the truck's big engine had enough power, even while simply idling, to move the car forward. With the steering wheel turned the way it was, it immediately began a sharp right turn. It had about eight feet to go before the front right tire left the roadway. Another three feet, and it was without footing as the hill sloped away quickly. From here, gravity did the rest, and the entire vehicle was soon sprinting down the steep hill at a pace slowed down by an occasional shrub or small tree.

The truck traveled 300 feet before it came to a sharp and fiery stop at the bottom of the ravine. During the plummet, Cha's door had closed, and Williamson saw the old man's frail body dancing about the cab until the sharp stop. Then, he saw it propelled out the front window and onto the shallow upslope on the opposite side of the ravine. From such a distance, Williamson couldn't be certain that Baker was dead, but the odds were pretty damn good.

He stood and watched for a few more minutes, but saw no movement below. Later tonight, more snow would fall, covering the wreck for another few days, but his work was done. He spat down the hillside toward Baker as a manner of salute.

44

State highways 53 and 41 intersect at the railroad crossing, separating the two main parts of town. Here, 53 would turn east, and 41 continued northeast, so if you were on 53 on the west side of Rathdrum and stayed driving straight, you'd switch to 41 without any effort. Highway 41 headed into the wildlands of northern Idaho, away from "big cities" like Westwood. From here, there were only a few small towns between Westwood and the Canadian border. If you get past the logging operations and hunting camps, a person could wander unseen by humans for days or weeks. It was one of those patches of the Inland Northwest where black bears still roamed, and more than one errant hiker or hunter had walked into the area and was never seen again. This is where Williamson headed.

His family had logged and hunted in these woods for decades, and he knew every back road. Whenever a search team was needed for any county, state, or federal operation, Williamson was called because of his intimate knowledge of the valleys, rivers, and ridges spanning Washington, Idaho, Montana, and Canada. He knew where many bodies had been located, and he knew exactly where to place them so no one could find their remains.

He'd prefer to go even further north, but that would take an extra couple of hours each way. Hours he didn't have. Now that he had killed Husted, his plans had to change. Initially, he didn't need to be at the noon meeting, but having killed a cop, his needs changed. If he had had the time, he'd have stuck with his original idea to take Gillum's body further up to an area about twenty miles north of Oldtown in the Colville National Forest. That area held vast tracts of old-growth forests untouched by man, with countless never-explored gullies and ditches.

Instead, he headed to an area closer to town but still just as untouched. As he reached Spirit Lake, he turned left onto Maine Street and headed through the still-sleeping town. Where the road crossed the small bridge over the lake, it became Spirit Lake Road and wound along the lakeside. It was slow going here, thanks to the dark, winding roads. There were patches of ice everywhere, so he drove extra carefully. Another mile along, past all the seasonal and resort homes of the snowbirds, another change in name. Here, it became Brickel Road, and most of the trees and land were owned by two different paper companies. There was no active logging here, and there hadn't been any for several years. It had been over-harvested, and the state and federal agencies overseeing such things had put an end to any work here for the foreseeable future. The paper companies made a show of planting new seedlings now and then, but it was basically barren of humans year-round.

There were dozens of logging trails in these hills, and Williamson knew each and every one. He grew up on these roads. He'd ride shotgun with his father and other family members or friends, and when he grew older, one of his first jobs was running loads out of these very mountains and back to the mills. Today, he wasn't taking a load. He was delivering one.

Though only a few miles on a map, the drive from Spirit Lake took almost an hour until he turned north onto a smaller logging road a mile short of the Washington border. Not far now. From the already minor road he was on, he turned west onto an even narrower one and made for the border, but stopped short of it by a quarter-mile. Just after he passed a small meltwater runoff stream, he braked his truck. He knew there'd be no traffic out here, but he still hurried to get out of these hills.

He sat quietly in the cab for a minute, reviewing what he needed to do. After a few deep breaths, he put on a small hiking headlamp and got out to begin his dirty work. Patches of snow and ice covered the ground, so his boots made a heavy crunch with each step. He reached over the side of the truck bed and removed the wood and tarp covering Husted. When clear, he went to the tailgate and lowered it. Grabbing the dead cop's ankles, Williamson smoothly but firmly pulled him out until he was clear of the bed. The body hit the frozen ground with a solid, disrespectful thud.

Williamson dragged Husted a few feet further away from the truck and began stripping him. Anything that would burn went into one pile, and he put anything that could not burn into another: badge, phone, keys, and his service weapon. When Husted was in nothing but socks and underwear, Williamson grabbed the kid by the ankles again and began dragging him to the downhill side of the road.

Because of the years of logging, there weren't many trees here, but the undergrowth had grown back thickly, making for a tough drag. The slush and snow hindered him further, but he stopped as he approached one of the dozens of huge slash piles that dotted the hillside. As part of the cleanup of timber harvests, the wood is collected and piled into these sizable mounds. Timber companies had teams that roamed their land in the fall and spring to set the piles aflame. There was enough moisture in late winter and early spring to prevent stray flames from spreading. About seventy-five feet down, he left the body by the side of the slash pile, which was next to a slowly trickling runoff stream. He headed back uphill.

He panted as he dragged Gillum from his cab to the same spot where he had stripped Husted and repeated the process on him. Another scramble down the hill, and he had the two in what could be mistaken in the dark for a lovers' embrace. Back at his truck, he grabbed the mallet and the canvas tarp. He stopped for a minute to catch his breath and steel himself before going downhill again.

There, he turned each body onto its back, giving him easy access to their faces. Taking a corner of the tarp, he laid it over Husted's face enough to cover it but not so much that Williamson couldn't see the position of the head. Making sure the tarp covered the face well, he reached down with his left hand, placed it on the forehead, and took a firm grip with the mallet in his right. Another deep breath, and Williamson swung hard to the left side of Husted's face. He hit twice more in the same area, then switched to the kid's other side. Using an opposite grip from before, Williamson gave three solid hits to the right side of the jaw and pulled the tarp back to see the results. As expected, it was a mess of blood, bone, and gore. He reached down to collect as many loose teeth as he could find and tossed them as far down the hill as possible. He knew he didn't need all of them, but he did need to ensure that he had done enough damage to remove any sense of a bite pattern.

Covering Husted's face again, he gave two more hits on each side to loosen the teeth even more. This did the trick. Williamson reached into the mess, retrieved all the loose teeth, and picked a few more off the ground, tossing them down the hill with the others. He then dragged the body as close to the pile of wet wood as possible.

Gillum received the same treatment. This time, though, he swung harder because of what he learned by hitting Husted's dead face. Teeth collected and strewn, he dragged the other body on top of the other. After looking around once more for any stray teeth, he headed uphill yet again.

From the truck bed, he grabbed an armful of kindling and the kerosene can. These were going to be the hardest trips. He wasn't a young man, and it had been a long day already. Going downhill with the kindling was bad enough, but going back up for the fourth time, even without a load, would be rough. He figured he'd have at least two trips down with the tamarack.

The final four trips took almost twenty-five minutes, but he was finally down by the pile with the bodies, kindling, kerosene, leaf blower, and the trash bag full of burnable items. He rested for a few minutes before arranging the kindling and wood into a pile atop the bodies. After finally catching his breath, he doused the new pile with the two gallons of kerosene and lit it with a flame from his Zippo lighter.

He let the fuel do its work while he moved to the older pile and began bringing small logs and slash from it onto his new pile. The wood he brought would light without a problem, but for his plan to work, he needed to get the wet wood burning, too. With several of the snowy logs placed, he sat back for a few more minutes to rest, but he still wasn't done.

Grabbing the leaf blower, he positioned its nozzle near the bottom of the pile, directing the airstream toward the heart of the flames. Because of the tight space within the pile, the influx of dry air created a blast furnace, heating the pile's interior far more than usual. After a few minutes, the extra heat and air dried the old logs, and they caught fire easily. Williamson shifted the blower's nozzle now and then to help spread the warmth and dryness to other wet areas, but he was sure the whole thing would be a glorious pyre within an hour. It would smolder and smoke, but that smoke would mingle in the air with the dozens of other slash piles lit in the area by private landowners and farmers.

Even if another snow came, the center embers would hold, and the fire would stay alive. By the time it died, the true springtime melt would begin, washing away whatever didn't burn in the fire.

Williamson sat on a rock, admiring his work for a few minutes longer. He'd had this idea in mind for years, this DIY crematorium, and it oddly satisfied him how well it turned out. He was sorry about Husted but consoled himself that he had simply gotten in the way. The old cop stood slowly, his muscles tired and tightening. The last, long trudge up the hill was the most difficult yet, but as he crested the roadside, he felt as excited as if he had climbed Mt. Rainier. One more killing, and he might get out of this mess.

45

Despite a mild hangover, I awoke promptly at 5:30 again. After taking some aspirin and water, I got up to pee, returned to bed, and fell back asleep just as quickly.

Just short of 7:00, my phone rang long enough and loud enough to wake me from this second round of slumber. It was the chief. I answered. "What's up?"

"I've got a missing cop," she said hurriedly into the phone. "You know anything about it?"

It was way too early after waking to be able to string cohesive thoughts together properly, so all I could answer was a simple no.

"Wait!" I sat up in bed, hoping the action would clear my head. "Who's missing? Williamson?"

"No. Husted!" she replied. "He was on graves and was last heard on the radio at two-fifteen. He checked in again after he made a foot patrol around the high school. We found his car on the other side of town."

She told me where, and by then I had woken enough to realize the patrol car was a couple of blocks from The Deadhead. Was there a connection? "Chief! We gotta talk," I said. "You at the shop? I can be there in twenty minutes."

Twenty-two minutes later, Hannah buzzed me in. Even the admin staff had been called in early. Sanchez was on the phone when I stepped into her office. "What's up?" I asked after she hung up.

"What's up is that I have zero information other than what I said on the phone," she said, and her exasperation was showing in how firmly she was holding her phone. I was worried she was going to crush it. "We have nothing other than his car and the radio check-in near two-thirty. I've got most of our officers on the road going over every street in town, and County has cars doing the same outside Westwood. Post Falls and Coeur d'Alene PDs are apprised and may send some units our way if needed. Spokane County has been notified, and they've got extra eyes on their side. I couldn't get a hold of my state contact yet, but I've called the dispatch center commander, and she got a bulletin out to everyone in the area. If anyone sees anything, we'll know right away, but so far, we have absolutely nothing. He hasn't gone home, and he doesn't seem to have contacted anyone. His girlfriend was waiting at home for him, but she says that she's heard nothing."

I wasn't sure what to add except, "Is his personal car still parked here?"

"Yes. Long went through it already. Nothing interesting or helpful. We went through his gear bag, locker, and the area where he usually sits. Nothing!" After a moment, she added, "Fuck!"

"What did you need to tell me?" she said after another pause.

"I went to The Deadhead last night and I—" Sanchez interrupted me.

"You went to The Deadhead?! No cops go to that shithole to drink. Only to arrest the beat-up bodies of anyone who loses their fight. How did Tony treat you?"

I hadn't heard the name before, but assumed it was the bartender. He looked like a Tony. "About as well as you'd expect. He seemed lovely. Anyway, in the short time I was there, I saw Williamson and someone who I'm guessing was Gillum seated together, looking like they were in deep discussion. Gillum took off soon after I sat down, but Williamson stayed for another minute or so to eyeball me and to make it look like they weren't leaving together. We didn't share a word. Just a smile and a nod."

"Where'd they go after that?" she asked excitedly.

"I don't know. I stayed to finish my drink and headed back to The Rathdrum. Funny thing, though. I must have such a trustworthy face that Tony felt comfortable enough to tell me all about what he and a fellow inmate did to a guard who pissed them off while they were living at Deer Lodge. That's the Montana Pen, I assume, and not a summer camp."

"You are correct. It's just down the road. I'll bet that you wanted to stay and get into a fight, ya troublemaking bastard."

"The thought crossed my mind, but one per day was enough. Plus, my energy level was down after the adrenaline dump from earlier. So I stayed all peaceful and shit."

I said the last part with a smile. Peaceful was rarely a word that could apply to me, and Sanchez knew it. The rest of the world hadn't seen what a softie I'd become with the chickens.

"Take a wild guess at which officer I couldn't get a hold of to come in. I'll give you a hint." She paused. "It's Williamson."

I couldn't put together what it all might mean. Williamson's absence may have an explanation. It was his weekend, after all, but Husted's absence was a big concern. Was he somehow connected to the mill or to Gillum as well?

"You'll probably have your hands full today," I noted. "Will you be able to swing by the mill at twelve?"

"Hadn't even thought of it until now," she said honestly. "I suppose that I'll be busy with all this shit. Even if Husted shows up now, there'll be some hell to pay."

"Just throwing this out there," I said conspiratorially, "but how about you call Gillum and tell him you won't be able to swing by. See how he reacts."

Sanchez thought out loud for a moment and said to no one, "There was nothing to lose on this. If I were magically able to swing by, it'd spook him even further. Maybe I'd ask him about Williamson, too, just to sense his reaction."

While I waited, she called. Nothing. Straight to voicemail. She didn't leave a message. She called the mill, thinking that maybe he'd come in already. Gail, the office manager, said he wasn't there and had texted last night that he wasn't coming in today.

She tried his cell phone once again, but it went to voicemail. Her next call was to Officer Long. He picked up right away. "What's your twenty right now?" she said quickly and with no pretense.

"I'm on 4th near Stub Meyer Park." He had been assigned the residential areas on the west side of town.

"I need you to do a welfare check." She gave him Gillum's address and hung up. "It should take him about five minutes to get there," she said to no one in particular.

I chimed in, "Where was his car found again?"

"In the parking lot of the gas station on Fifty-three and Bingham. He didn't call out for a traffic stop or a foot patrol. Husted has spent too much time with Williamson, so he doesn't always report when he's out of his car. I've been on his ass about that, but he'd definitely call in for a traffic stop."

"If it were for a foot patrol, what would he be checking? Houses or businesses?" I spent enough time on patrol to know the value of being on foot, silently walking through a neighborhood. It could be time-consuming and often led to nothing, but it was an intimate way to "feel" the streets.

"There are only a few businesses there, but there's usually a few trucks parked along Fifty-three. We've had tweakers steal shit right off the rig while the drivers were sleeping," she said this with a hint of amusement. The brazenness with which people would risk their lives to make a few bucks still amazed her.

She continued, "Every one of those drivers was packing heat, and every cop knew it. It was expected. The tweakers didn't know or didn't care. Every six months or so, there would be a dead body found shot in a truck turnoff, most likely killed by a trucker defending his rig. The loss of life was sad, but few cops put much effort into solving the crime."

From the speaker on her desk, they heard Long call out at Gillum's address. They waited again.

"No answer at the front door, but there's a car here." He called in the plates to the dispatcher to check for the registered owner. It belonged to Gillum. "Going around back."

In the office, the play-by-play was riveting. Odds were nothing would happen, but every cop who'd ever been in this situation was waiting for some sign that something would go bad and they'd need to react—but not yet.

"No answer, but it's unlocked. Going in." Long knew that a welfare check meant they could go in without a warrant to make sure the resident was all right. Any crime uncovered was incidental, but there could be no thorough search. Just make sure the person is okay and get out.

After a tense two minutes, Long said into his mic, "Clear! No one here. Going out the front door."

The chief's phone rang immediately, and she answered it on speaker. It was Long. "The place is a mess, but no signs of struggle. His bed was slept in, but I didn't see his keys or phone anywhere."

"Okay," she said, "get out of there, but scour that area again. Lots of back roads and trails out of the backside of that neighborhood."

"Will do, Chief." Long hung up without ceremony.

"Well, fuck!" I said. "That's another wrinkle. What now?"

"Now we keep sniffing around and wait for a break." She didn't seem happy about waiting, but there wasn't much she could do other than what she already had her team doing. When the city attorney calls back, she'll finish up the warrants for Husted's phone records and credit card activity. If either had been used, it would have given her some hope. Until then, it was slow going ahead.

"I'm useless here," I said. "I'll stay out of the way, but I want to go to where he was parked and walk around. I'd like to see what Husted may have seen."

"Sure, but stay cool. Let me know where you're at, and keep me updated if you find anything interesting."

"Will do, Supe!"

46

It would have been easy to cross the tracks near the station, but I'd seen too many bodies mutilated by trains down in Kansas City not to respect how those giant, loud machines still manage to sneak up on people and snuff them out. Instead, I walked the extra few feet to Mill Street to get to 53. There, I stayed on the south side of the highway and walked along the now-empty shoulder where trucks had parked last night and will again tonight. I focused on the ground and the road edge where the gravel turned to weeds, looking for any hint of a disturbance. A few minor fluid stains from the trucks and more cigarette butts than there should be, but nothing new or out of place.

I stayed on that side of the highway until I reached the end of the turnout, right across from the lot where Husted had parked his car. A flatbed had already come to remove the cruiser, but I could still see four marks painted on the ground where it had been. I moved toward the liquor store across the street from the gas station, planning to work up the block to the car lot before heading back. The car lot was also a mechanic shop, with an even mix of used cars ready for sale and damaged cars awaiting repairs. There seemed to be one person inside the office, but because it was Saturday, the repair shop was closed. Trying to draw as little attention as possible, I wove through the cars for sale and continued searching the ground.

I worked my way back to the gas station, but not before swinging behind and around the liquor store across the street. I continued walking the path as if on a night patrol, but in daylight, my focus was different. At night, you're listening and smelling as much as you're seeing. In the daylight, the visual cues and horrors were plain to the naked eye.

As natural as it was for me to be doing this, I was not too fond of it. I'd much rather be back at the farm sipping coffee and watching the girls peck and scratch in the morning sun. This was too much like what drove me away from police work in the first place: tracking down another dead body or evidence of human sin and malice.

With the Deadhead closed and no cars present, I took a lap around the building's rear, paying close attention to its dumpster. Had Husted come by here, it would have been after the bar had closed. Maybe he disturbed a nighttime transaction of some kind, but I couldn't find any evidence of a struggle or commotion. I continued southwest along the highway. Beginning at the gas station, I backtracked several times to cover every paved area on this side of the road. At night, they would have been the safest places to walk.

I weaved along and around the bead shop and checked thoroughly behind the old cafe on the corner of 53 and McCartney Street. Here, the tree cover became thicker, and a runoff ditch ran behind the businesses. The East Greenacres Main Ditch began here and served as the catchment for the rain and snowmelt that accumulated in the neighborhood. While still early in spring, the ditch had an icy trickle this morning, but within a couple of weeks, it would flow strongly with snowmelt from the hills and gullies surrounding Rathdrum Mountain. I inspected the area but made a mental note to come back soon to walk the ditch downstream.

Coming out of the wooded area where the ditch passed under McCartney Street, I stepped onto the asphalt and headed toward the stop sign across the roadway. Twenty feet from the sign and in the middle of the street, I found what I hoped not to find. Though still shaded by the trees ahead, the low morning sun was enough to reveal two distinct spots on the ground that shone differently from the surrounding area. As I drew closer, I saw that the shapes were distinct from one another, yet both bore the same blood-red hue. The roadway was mostly dry, but the cold kept the blood from drying or spreading too much. The droplets had lost some of their form, but enough remained to let any half-trained observer know what they were. One only had to look for it.

With my phone, I snapped three pictures: one of each bloodstain and one more of the street sign showing the intersection. I sent them to Sanchez in a text, with no accompanying message. She would get the idea.

Be there in 3.

47

I heard her car before I saw it. Chief Sanchez was as good as her word; she pulled up to block the intersection in less than four minutes. She jumped out of the car, leaving its lights on. Oliviera was less than two minutes behind, and she pulled up at the intersection of McCartney and Post Street.

While waiting for the chief, I snapped a few photos of the asphalt and grass on the west side of the intersection. The sun would soon hit the area, and any marks or mars in the ice or moisture would disappear quickly. There was nothing of note worth seeing, but it was still standard, even if you're not a cop anymore.

Sanchez was still a cop, though. And the chief on top of that. One of her boys was missing, and the newly discovered bloodstains made her fear the worst. She'd lost fellow officers before, brothers and sisters in blue, but now this missing cop was hers. Her cop. Her brother and son. She strode from her car to me, and I quickly picked up on her heightened mood. She was all business, and I obliged.

"I was walking from the ditch to the intersection." I pointed over to the runoff ditch behind the cafe on the other side of the street, "and saw the reflections. I came within a few feet and stopped when I figured out what it was." Again, I pointed, this time to a spot a few feet north of the stains. "At that point, I took the three pictures that I sent you and stepped away. Since then, I've only walked on the far side of the road." I pointed again, this time to the asphalt at the entrance to the cafe's parking lot. I told her about the extra photos I'd taken of the asphalt and the grass, and she had me send them to her right then. My report was concise yet complete. It gave the chief everything I knew up to that point and told her which parts of the crime scene I might have contaminated.

Oliviera was halfway from her car to us when the chief stopped her with an upraised hand. "Collection kit and camera," she said. The detective stopped immediately and returned to her car's trunk to retrieve them. Sanchez grabbed her lapel mic and was about to make a call, but stopped when she saw another patrol unit crossing the tracks and turning toward her. It was Officer Long. She pointed emphatically into the cafe's parking lot, and Long understood that he was to park there. He got out and headed toward the chief at the same time that Oliveira came close again. She spoke to them both, "Pictures of everything, then a sample of both puddles." She turned to Long. "Take them to the medical center for typing. Take no shit from anyone. Call ahead to have them ready, and I'll have Husted's records checked so they can match."

Long nodded, but Oliveira, another Army veteran, curtly said, "Hoo-uh," and moved on to her mission. Sanchez pulled out her phone and made a call. It went to voicemail, but I quickly realized it was for the city attorney. "Tammy, I'll have two warrant applications for you within the hour. One for Barry Gillum's home and the other for Husted's. Call me if there are any problems."

As soon as she hung up, she said to Oliviera, "Get on those warrants as soon as you're done here." Without waiting for a response, she turned to me. "Who was around when you found these? Which cars were in the lot?"

"There was no traffic about and no one in that lot." I nodded toward the church parking lot west of the intersection. "I didn't see anyone in the cafe, but the lights were on. Three cars in the lot: those two trucks and the minivan. No one or nothing else."

"Okay. Long, you take off as soon as you've got the samples. I'm going inside to check if anyone saw anything." She strode off without further comment and without waiting for permission. She was a chief in charge and in a groove. No one was going to get in her way.

Long went over to his detective, leaving me standing alone in a blood-stained intersection in a town with possibly two more dead souls.

48

Williamson could feel the fatigue in his bones, but he had no time to rest. The transfer was less than an hour away, not enough time for him to head home. He'd have to go there later to pack. Killing Husted changed everything. He was insulated from Cha and his murders, and he thought that there was enough distance between him and Gillum that he might be free of that stink, but Warren probably fucked that up when he saw them together at the bar. The chief now had Gillum linked to the girl. *Fuck it all*, he thought as he looked down at his phone to see yet another incoming call from the station. He ignored this one, too. There was no point in picking up now.

A thorough internal investigation would follow, uncovering links to the mill and to extra payments in and out, some to Williamson, some to other cops and deputies. The decision to kill Husted was swift, but it was the right one. Perhaps there was some regret, but after reflection, he decided he wouldn't miss the rookie. In fact, once he left town, he wouldn't miss anyone at all. He only had to survive the next few hours, and he could escape.

He had a place waiting for him in Montana. That, his brothers in the militia, and a shitload of cash would help him live off the grid for quite a while. Comfortably, too.

The cab of his truck wasn't perfectly clean, but it would do. Before burning the clothing, he had used

Gillum's t-shirt to wipe up the few blood splatters that were inside the cab. He washed off the few drops of Husted's blood on the outside of the truck with a water bottle he had and splashed some kerosene over the area to ruin any DNA evidence that remained. He poured a little more kerosene on Gillum's T-shirt, wiped down the cab where the blood had pooled, then set the shirt with the other items to burn. Not perfect, but it would pass a quick visual inspection. It only needed to hold for a few more hours anyway.

When he pulled into the mill's lot, Mallard's Jeep was already there, parked outside the garage shed. Before Williamson even stopped his truck, Mallard was outside, and he looked pissed. "Where the hell have you been? I've been packing all this shit by myself!"

Williamson strode toward the older man, cool on the surface but feeling exhausted. "There was a small hiccup taking care of Gillum."

This froze Mallard, who'd been so busy being upset about doing the work himself, along with the stress of transfer day, that perhaps he had forgotten about having ordered the man's death. "Oh," he said, almost embarrassed. "All good?" He knew better than to ask detailed questions for which he didn't want answers.

"All good," Williamson said without making eye contact. "Let's get to it." He strode past Mallard and headed into the shed. They had less than an hour to get ready.

Inside the garage shed was a cargo container. Inside the cargo container were seven steel 55-gallon drums labeled "hazardous materials". Inside those drums was the accumulated inventory of non-timber-related products from the various deliveries they had received in the past month.

Mallard used a spreadsheet to track every ounce of product entering the yard. He had to. There was so much money at stake, but more importantly, any shortage of product would be fatal. He had finally found a way to make this mill profitable and didn't want to jeopardize it. Get the shipments in from the Ukrainians, store them for a few days or weeks, get paid by the Irish guys, take your proper cut, and get the rest back to the "family" and be done with it. Don't skim. Don't lose any product.

Williamson understood that Mallard never skimmed because he valued his good arrangement. He had never lost any product, maintaining a close-knit circle. Until now, he had never faced police scrutiny. Cha had established an effective system ten years ago, and Gillum had managed to avoid disrupting it—at least until now. Williamson and Mallard knew Gillum wasn't very smart, but he was loyal and kept quiet most of the time. Williamson saw the older man shake his head, perhaps to clear his thoughts. They needed to work quickly to load the pallets. Mallard had already prepared the three pallets they would use, lining them with the first layer of fifty-pound bags of stove pellets.

49

I was deadweight at this point in the search for Husted and Gillum. The chief had to have sensed it, too, but was too polite to say anything. After processing the scene where the stains were found, they all returned to the station to continue managing and monitoring the search, and I immediately felt out of place. The missing cop was one of them, and I wasn't. Even Sanchez was cool and distant toward me. It was time to go, and I had to find a polite way out.

"Chief, unless you need me for something, I'm gonna get out of the way," I said in her office. There was a look of mild relief on her face. She hadn't wanted to kick me out, but she also knew I could do no good now. I wasn't one of her officers she could use in the search, merely a civilian who could get in the way.

"Yeah, that'd be best for now," she said with a slight air of apology. "You're a bump on a log at this point. Fuller said his team will be done with your place in a few more hours. My guys are done in the shed, so you can have it back later today. I'll give you…" she paused. "Shit. No one was there to let the kids out this morning. I'll call Fuller and have him…"

"Nah! Let him finish." I jumped at the chance. "I'll swing by and do it. I miss the girls. Give him a call or text to say I'm coming by. I'll stay out of his way, and I won't go in the house until you give the green light." It was a great way to escape this feeling of uselessness and see my girls again.

The CR-V was in the back lot of the hotel waiting for me, and I wasted no time heading toward my place and the kids. The morning layer of mist had worn off, and the gentle winds had cleared most of the sky of the cloud cover from earlier. Despite all the madness of the previous few days, my mind was relatively calm on the drive home. It would be a quick visit, but it still filled me with a sense of peace to be back on the dirt. My dirt. Though within a few miles of town, it almost seemed like another world—flat prairie in three directions with few distant houses and barns to intrude. As I made the last turn onto my road, I saw that one of the Powells was out in the field directly south of my place, working on a stone harvest. Hope he finds nothing but stones and dirt.

I pulled into the driveway and parked next to Fuller's van, but before heading in, I turned around and watched the young man. It looked like Randall, the eldest boy, had stopped the four-wheeler and tractor to collect more stones.

BAM!

BAM!

BAM!

Each one announced itself loudly as it hit the metal of the trailer bed. Though the low clouds weren't there today to amplify and echo the sound, it was still plenty loud enough to be heard for miles on the calm, quiet prairie.

"Fuck!" I said softly. I hadn't known it until now, but I had discovered a new trigger noise. My calm mood turned melancholy. The sound of stone on metal was distinctive. I now knew that for the rest of my life, that sound would portend or foretell impending death. I had my own field to finish harvesting, a field that had yielded a bumper crop of dead women.

I shook my head and headed to the coop, where the kids waited. On the way, I waved to Fuller out in the field with his two teammates. The hens were inside the coop, and their energy showed. They had been scratching at the straw and gravel on the ground, and Big Red was atop the highest perch. When he saw me enter, he stretched himself tall and flapped his wings. I was happy that the bird didn't crow. That noise in this tiny space would have been overwhelming.

I made my way to the inner door of the coop and stepped through, making sure none of the kids escaped. I grabbed the red coffee container and sensed a wave of excitement from the hens. Scooping up a load of the bean-and-seed mix, I went back through the inner door, and the girls immediately swarmed at my feet. With the flock waiting on me, I continued through the coop and went out the other side. The coop and outer-pen doors were already open, but no one had yet left because the food was here. They followed every step of the way to the compost box, where I scattered the feed so the little dinosaurs could have at it.

Madness! Thirty-odd chickens scratched and fought their way through the compost and through each other to get to the feed—a primeval event; the basic hunt for survival. There was something admirable in it, a reminder of life's fundamental, base aspects. The little birds reminded me that all things have a biological purpose. Even humans do. Sometimes, though, I couldn't figure out what mine was. I had tried soldiering and being a cop. I made a reasonable effort to be a partner to a wonderful woman. Now I was worried that the farmer/nature boy phase of my life would be cut short by more death and human misery.

I wanted to go to Fuller to ask questions about the search, but I knew that would be inappropriate. I'd wait for the final report, the final body count. Instead, I turned and headed back to the barn to return the red bucket. The chickens ignored me as I went.

50

I entered the hotel through the back entrance and found the place had a modest crowd for breakfast. Murphy ran from table to table, bringing food or sometimes chatting with neighbors. Trapper Dan was at the bar, having breakfast of chicken-fried steak, gravy, and Budweiser. The older man saw me and raised his bottle in salute and greeting.

After swallowing, he said, "Whole town's gone to shit today. You have anything to do with that?" It wasn't an accusation, more like a friendly conversation starter.

"No," I replied, "I'm trying to stay out of the way."

"That's probably best." After a swig of Bud, he continued. "Any time you've got missing cops, it's best to stay low. Those in blue don't take kindly when theirs get hurt."

"You said 'cops' plural. It's only one missing at the moment."

"What about Williamson?" the old man said. "He hasn't been seen either. Folks are sayin' that Gillum finally got sick and tired of being treated like a little bitch by everyone, and that he finally snapped and grew a set of balls. Lord knows he'd allowed himself to be treated like shit his whole life. His parents, his wife, Cha, Mallard. Everyone! Folks are sayin' he'd had enough."

A stray thought about the disappearances of Husted and Williamson crossed my mind, but I brushed it off as improbable. Instead, I prodded Trapper Dan.

"Which folks are sayin' this?" I asked with a healthy dose of skepticism.

"Well, me," Dan said with a hint of humility. "I'm sayin'. I never liked that little runt of a cocksucker."

Murphy came around the bar to save me from more of Dan's small-town shit-talking. "Howdy. Karl. What's new? What can I get for ya?"

I pointed over to Dan's plate. "That looks perfect. That and a Bud, please." The thick country gravy looked enticing, especially mixed in with the fried potatoes and green beans on the plate. I was hungrier than I thought.

"Damnit, Dan!" Murphy said. "You're infecting my nicest customer." He said it as a half-joke. The other half wasn't. "There you go, kid." He placed the bottle on the bar and headed off to place the order.

I let Dan eat in peace, but my mind was now going over the possibilities of what had happened over the last day. I could see the highlights, but there were still missing pieces. Dead girls, EPA violations, missing mill employees, a secret romance, a dirty cop, and some sort of drug transaction. Had Husted not gone missing, the chief might have been able to shake something loose at the mill today. Instead of being there at noon, she was chasing a missing cop and a missing mill employee, wondering where Williamson was.

She was busy. She was busy and couldn't be at the mill. The timing of the disappearances was perfect if one wanted to have some privacy.

I looked at the clock to check the time: 10:35. Enough time for breakfast and to get to the mill to see what's happening at twelve. I turned to Dan.

"Hey! Where does Williamson live?"

248

51

The chicken-fried steak was perfect and made my belly happy. The three beers had helped take the edge off, too, but at the same time, they filled me with a drop of shame. I knew better. Now wasn't the time to worry about that, though.

I parked my Honda on a small turnout along the road behind the amusement park and, after grabbing a small pack from the passenger seat, walked the old road to the back side of the mill and the gate I had seen the previous day. Before approaching, I moved into the woods a hundred feet away from the gate. I hadn't heard any noise or commotion coming from the yard, but I wanted to find a good overwatch spot before getting too close. That task proved easy enough, as I found a good overgrown area along the fenceline that let me see the garage shed and the side of the office I hadn't seen yesterday.

Williamson's truck was parked beside a Jeep, but I saw no activity. The shed's bay doors were open, and I could see the front end of the Ford truck from yesterday. Nothing else. No sign of people. I checked my phone. 11:25. No service on this side of the mill. Nothing to do but wait until noon to see what happens.

There was a clear space on the ground near a ninebark bush, and I made myself comfortable at its base. The wind carried the faint musk of skunk, either from afar or up close; I couldn't tell. It was an unpleasant smell, yet one with warm memories attached to it from days gone by.

I was the third of three children, three sons, and I'd always known as if, by the time my parents got around to having me, five years after the middle child, they were simply tired of parenting and put less effort into me. Once, on a rafting trip on one of the many rivers feeding into the Lake of the Ozarks, my father took my two brothers on a special side trip, a hike into the woods to find an old settlement cabin, leaving me with my mother.

I knew they left me behind because I was too young and would slow them down, but I wanted to go along anyway. My mother had me help tidy the lakeside campsite and prepare the meal for their return, yet I spent most of my time sitting in the tall grass and among the wildflowers. I watched the insects crawl, jump, and fly from leaf to stem and flower, and back again, as jet boats sped by and houseboats floated lazily.

The noise my brothers and father made tromping along the trail announced their return at camp before the sight of them did, as did their smell. On their hike, a mama skunk protecting her kits from the perceived threat posed by the Warrens had sprayed them. Apparently, my eldest brother startled a young skunk, shrieking in his excitement, which brought my father and other brother just in time to be gassed by the now-alerted mother skunk.

While I didn't enjoy being so close to such a strong and unpleasant smell, it was a small piece of justice for being left behind on the side adventure. Since then, the scent of skunk has always brought a smile and a warm recollection.

Back in the present, from the small pack, I pulled out binoculars and a sixteen-ounce can of beer that I bought at the gas station before I left Westwood—time to kill some time.

52

Were it not an unofficial stakeout on private property, trying to help figure out the mystery behind a great number of murders, new and old, I might have enjoyed the time in the woods. Though it was late morning, with the sun high, it was pleasant and calm in the shade of the pines. Spring hadn't quite sprung yet, but there were a few signs of its impending arrival. The unseen birds in the trees and shrubs were busy and loud, and in the sunny patches where the ice and snow had already melted, a few of the grass clumps shot forth new, green spikes to the sky.

Unfortunately, as wonderful as the spot was, it didn't keep my mind occupied, and I needed a distraction from stray thoughts. I rechecked the phone, but I still wasn't in range of a cell tower here. Maybe a half-mile in any direction or way over in the mill's parking lot, but not behind the yard. I was alone with my thoughts. This rarely turned out well.

One of the first things that crossed my mind was an old classic: Why? Why am I sitting in the woodline? Why am I not back at the bar? Why did I get myself wrapped up in all this bullshit? The surrounding silence was enough of an answer because I already knew why.

Since childhood, I've had to confront danger to protect others. A more appropriate question would be why it had taken me so long to get back in the game. The pile of death and misery in Kansas City grew so large that I thought I'd had enough of this life. What I definitely had enough of was the human misery, the hatred humans shared toward one another, and the horrible deeds they committed against one another.

Years ago, I heard a story about a nomadic hunter from a few thousand years ago. He had spent a long day hunting for his clan. His fruits were modest, but he could head back with a few rabbits and birds he had surprised. Though it was getting late, he wanted to take a few minutes to enjoy the colors of the setting sun. Taking a seat on a large flat rock, the hunter made himself comfortable as the sun blanketed the sky with its array of yellows, oranges, reds, purples, and blues. The hunter was pleased. He had been successful enough that he could fill the bellies of his clan tonight, and he had taken a moment to enjoy the natural world around him.

That moment is when the tiger jumped from a higher rock onto the unsuspecting nomad and killed him. The lesson of the story always eluded me, but the old sergeant who told it to me years ago seemed to make it about not being too proud and always staying alert. Regardless, I often think of the tiger anytime I'm in the woods and enjoying myself too much.

Back in Kansas City, while on lunch breaks or slow periods, my fellow officers often teased me for being ultra-alert, even during my downtime. I'd park in the safest spaces, always keep my back to a wall, and always make sure that I could see all the avenues of approach. Sure, most cops did this, but I did this to an almost hyper-religious degree. Perhaps it's the same reason that I appreciated Big Red so much. That damn rooster rarely took any downtime. He had a flock to protect and took his mission seriously, but here I was in the Idaho wilderness, admiring the grass shoots and sunbeams, waiting for the tigers to pounce on me.

Shame sifted through me as I thought of all I had given up by leaving, but I made the right choice. I had bottomed out emotionally and had no desire to spend one more day driving through the city, anticipating the next death or bout of hatred from its populace. I had long given up the idea of having a social life in the town. Toward the end of my time with Laura, I had already been too uptight and irritable to enjoy time out on dates, and after her departure, there was even less reason to step out socially. I felt trapped. Had I not found the money, I might not have made such an escape. I'd probably have either eaten my gun by now or gotten fired for cause.

I missed the chickens. I missed the porch. I missed morning coffee. How am I going to feel good about my place knowing that all those dead girls had been marinating there for all these years?

"Fuck!" I said to the birds in the trees. They said nothing in return.

The truck's engine announced itself before I saw it. As soon as it turned onto the gravel road to the mill, I heard its wheels crunching on the ground, but didn't see it until it turned into the yard from the lot. The truck was old, maybe as old as 1970, but it was a beauty—a white GMC thirteen-ton flatbed with dual rear tires—a dinosaur, but still running strong. As soon as it came into the yard, Williamson and an older man, one of the men I saw unloading trucks yesterday, came out of the shed. I assumed it was Mallard. I saw two men in the truck's cab, and it didn't stop in front of the shed. Instead, it stayed about fifty feet away and parked with its nose directly facing the two men waiting for it.

The driver was the first to step out of the cab. As he left the truck, he grabbed a pistol from underneath the seat and kept it in his right hand at his side before walking toward Williamson and Mallard. Then I noticed Williamson had a gun holstered on his right hip. It wasn't his police rig, but it looked serious enough. Driver came twenty feet from his welcoming committee and took a slow look around. After finishing an unknown mental security checklist, or simply when he was comfortable enough, he turned back to his passenger and gave one curt nod. Passenger stepped out and made a show of grabbing a sizable black bag from the truck. It was shaped like a gym bag, but the size of an airplane carry-on.

Mid-40s, 5'10", lean, and dressed in black, the man walked slowly toward his greeters with smooth, easy strides as if he'd made this walk a thousand times, like there was nothing unnatural about armed men meeting in a mill yard in Idaho on a Saturday afternoon. I could hear a muffled conversation, but at 200 feet, I couldn't make out any clear words. Mallard shook hands with Passenger, and they walked into the darkness of the garage shed. Williamson kept his eye on Driver with the pistol, but, after a minute, nodded to him as an invitation to come in if he wished.

I could see some commotion inside the shed, but nothing distinct. *Should I try to move closer?* I wanted to, but I couldn't see a path that wouldn't expose me to anyone in the shed. More waiting. More birdsong and whistles of the wind in the trees. More empty time for my mind to wander.

Breathe. Just breathe. At this moment, I couldn't do anything except worry and fret and fear and let the mind-monkeys holler. Or breathe. Just focus on the breath and the breeze. Stay vigilant and open to the world.

Nothing from the garage, but from the woods behind me, I distinctly heard the caw of ravens and the snare beat of a woodpecker. After ten minutes, nothing happened in the yard, and I couldn't hear any noise from the shed. This looked like a transfer, but what was being transferred? I assumed the bag held cash to pay for whatever was unloaded from Tuxedo and Flannel's truck yesterday. Drugs? Most likely. What does this have to do with the dead girls in my dirt?

Again, the wind and birdsong offered no answer, but before I could enjoy the silence again, Driver stepped out of the shed and headed toward his truck. He got in, started it, and made a wide turn to point its nose away from the shed, then stopped and backed up seventy-five feet. He got back out and joined Passenger, who had come into view while the truck was moving. I heard an engine rumble to life inside the shed, but whatever made the noise stayed where it was. Until it didn't.

Two minutes later, I saw the source of the sound: a propane-powered forklift exiting the shed with a fully loaded pallet on its forks. The load looked like a pile of bags, but they were all shrink-wrapped in plastic, so I couldn't be certain. Mallard, or who I assumed was him, placed the first load in the truck bed near the cab and, over the next five minutes, added two more pallets. The whole time, Williamson and Driver stood on either side of the truck, waiting for the other to cause trouble while slyly watching all the different corners of the yard. Passenger stood and watched and seemed as if he didn't have a care in the world, like he was waiting for his bus to arrive.

With the loading completed, Mallard drove the empty forklift back into the shed and returned a moment later to walk to the back of the truck. Driver and Passenger threw the load straps over the pallets, and Mallard helped get them nice and snug. Two straps on each load, and they weren't going anywhere. As soon as he secured the load, Driver climbed into the cab and fired up the engine. He was on a mission. Passenger spent a moment exchanging pleasantries with Mallard, then, with a handshake, bid farewell and got into the truck. Driver wasted no time in leaving. I saw the old GMC leave the yard and listened to its noise fade off into the Idaho afternoon.

Williamson and Mallard stood side by side, watching the truck disappear. They exchanged no words. The moment that the sound of the truck faded, Williamson pulled another pistol, this one with a suppressor, from inside his coat, turned to the stunned Mallard, and placed three quick shots into his shocked face and head. Mallard was dead instantly, but his body didn't get the message right away. After a moment, his knees gave out, and his dead flesh came down in a heap. Almost as soon as Mallard's body hit the ground, Williamson pulled what looked to be a napkin out of his pocket and bent down to pick up the three spent shells from the gravel and dirt. He wrapped them inside the napkin, placed them in his pants pocket, and returned the pistol to the inside coat pocket from which it came. He stood up and checked himself for blood splatter and, once satisfied, grabbed Mallard by the collar of his coat and dragged him the forty feet to the shed.

I sat in the dirt and grass without a radio, no cell service, and no weapon. I ran through a brief list of options, but before I could choose one, Williamson returned from the shed and headed for his truck and Mallard's Jeep. In his left hand was the black bag.

He walked to the Jeep, opened its driver's door, and tossed the bag inside. Walking quickly over to his truck, he pulled out a white plastic bag, but I couldn't tell what was inside it. Again walking quickly, he returned to the garage. No sound from his activity reached my distant position, but Williamson didn't give me too much time to get lonely. Within two minutes, he was outside again, headed to the Jeep. In another minute, he was gone, leaving nothing but a trail of dust on the gravel road.

53

It had to be now. Williamson thought to himself. *He's gonna put the bag in his safe, and I'll never see it again.* Mallard's fate had already been sealed, but until that moment, Williamson wasn't sure when it would happen. The Irish were gone, no one was at the mill, and the money case would be locked up soon. The bag was on a workbench inside the shed, but as soon as they came in to get it, Mallard would head for his safe. Now. Now!

Williamson reached in and grabbed the .22 from the inside pocket of his brown Carhartt coat. He flipped the safety off with his thumb before he pulled it out, and he wasted no time getting his feet into a shooting position because the tiny gun wouldn't kick much. He needed to get him cleanly so there would be no struggle. Three shots to his face and head, and it was done. Mallard didn't have time to react, his body showing no signs of recoiling from the sight of the gun or any reaction to the rounds from it.

Before he even loaded the weapon, Williamson wiped each round to remove fingerprints. He'd seen enough cases cracked because of shell casings being left at the scene and matched later. Always police your brass when you're trying to get away with murder. Always. Crime 101. He did so with a napkin, wadded it around the shells, and stuffed it in his pants pocket.

Mallard's body was easy enough to drag, and once inside the shed, Williamson grabbed Mallard's keys from his pocket and pulled the corpse into the container that had once stored drug shipments from Canada. Now it would be Mallard's tomb. He also tossed in the napkin with the shells. He grabbed the black bag and headed out to the Jeep. There, he placed the money, then returned to his truck to grab Husted's radio and the bag of everything he couldn't burn. Back inside the garage, he wiped down each unburnable item before tossing it into the container. Securing the handle and securing the lock, he grabbed the key seated in the base, wiping everything he'd touched. There was only one key, so if anyone wanted inside the container, they'd have better luck cutting through the side than sawing through that lock. He'd toss the key somewhere along the road. Williamson thought no one would open the container until the body smelled enough to penetrate its metal shell. *Not a perfect plan, but it'll hold for a day or so.*

Williamson gave a last look around the shed and, seeing nothing amiss, headed to Mallard's Jeep. He had another few hours and a couple of hundred miles to go today before he could relax, so it'd be better not to be seen in his own truck. He was sure he'd be getting some attention soon. One more stop at home, and he'd be free. Driving away from the mill, a slight wave of twisted pride washed over him. Three kills within eleven hours. *Cha would be proud*, he thought.

54

Though I had just watched a cold-blooded, pre-planned murder, it didn't raise my heartbeat at all. Somehow, the killing affected me less than a car horn, the crack of billiard balls, or an unexpected siren. Mallard's death seemed almost to be a normal progression of the story playing out in front of me. I knew I should call 911, but with no cell service, I was stranded. Williamson drove away in Mallard's Jeep, and the sound of the tires on the gravel road diminished.

I'd never been disillusioned about the sanctity or perfection of cops. I held them to a higher standard, and I'd know plenty that never came close to it. Hell! I stole millions from a crime scene. Other cops in the department did the same to a much lesser degree; some beat their wives or cheated on them. Some got too rough with their suspects, and we had more than one wrongful shooting. What I had witnessed was unlike anything I had ever seen. This was a straight-up, cold-blooded murder. Cold, calculated, planned, and executed. Mallard, if that's who that was, had no idea it was coming because he had trusted Williamson to be on the inside of his crime circle. There was no reason to mourn the loss of Mallard, an apparent major link in the drug chain, but seeing this killing confirmed the improbable thought that had been bouncing around in my head: Williamson had slain Husted. So many things were connected, and I was foolish for not realizing how much the old cop was involved in everything.

Sitting in the natural silence of the treeline, I felt warm and comfortable, despite Williamson's actions and despite the heavy thoughts swirling in my head. So comfortable, in fact, that for a moment, I considered the idea of doing nothing and going back to the town for lunch and maybe to get my dirt back from Fuller's guys. I'd have the girls back, too. Tempting, but I knew that I couldn't take that path. Instead, I would have to act in some way.

A memory of a nature program I had watched recently flashed to mind, this time narrated by George Page, another classic voice. A caiman was swimming peacefully in a river somewhere in the Amazon basin, enjoying its life, doing whatever caimans do during the daytime for leisure. This one was big, six feet, an adult male, perhaps well known in the reptile community for his good deeds and bad. None of that mattered to the jaguar that was waiting for it.

The jaguar wasn't concerned with what business the caiman had coming up later that day, what plans it had for life, whether there were little reptile spawn depending on it, or if it had a date later that night. Nothing mattered to that jaguar except that this particular one swam by its perch at a time of the jaguar's liking. With a silent leap, jaws-first onto the caiman's neck, the jaguar and prey disappeared under the brown water for a few seconds before the cat emerged with a mouthful of dinner. With power belied by the size difference between the smaller jaguar and its prey, the cat swam to shore, leaped up the bank, and disappeared into the thick forest underbrush.

In front of me, I had a few choices. I could drive west or south into cell range and call it in, or I could try to follow Williamson. I wasn't exactly sure what my next step was, but I had to move; otherwise, I might change my mind, drive back home, and let all of this go. Doing nothing was a realistic option.

Thinking about the jaguar, I went with a fourth option, a slightly different one, that might either shut down some of the ghosts and demons or make them come roaring back, stronger than ever, into my life. Grabbing my gear, I stood up and began a brisk, martial stride back to my Honda, my half-assed plan idea gelling as I walked. After six minutes, I could feel the first beads of sweat welling up on my back and neck. Once back in the car, instead of turning around and heading back to town, I drove north along the county road, taking the back roads to the small highway leading to Williamson's house.

55

Williamson liked Sanchez as a chief and appreciated her efforts to modernize the department, but one change he was glad hadn't been made yet was the purchase of new radios with built-in GPS. On those more modern radios, any call would also show the radio's location. The older radios the Westwood PD used lacked this feature. It was this trait that Williamson wanted to exploit.

Ten minutes after leaving the mill, his heart rate slowed, and he was more at ease. He had over three million dollars in cash on the seat next to him, a safe landing spot waiting for him in Montana, and was so close to being gone. The next step was stopping at home, but the end was near. Grabbing Husted's radio, he made a call that would give him even more breathing room.

Using a weak and panicked voice, he whispered into the mic, "County, Whiskey Papa 3-5. Officer Down!"

The dispatcher came back immediately with obvious interest in her voice. "Whiskey Papa 3-5, County. What's your location and status?"

"I'm shot. I'm on the back side of the Speedway. Close to the Valhalla gravel pit." Williamson knew this was as far away in the county from his house as possible. If he were in the dispatch room right now looking at the control board, he'd see the blinking lights indicating all the patrol cars headed toward Husted's supposed location, giving him extra time and space.

There hadn't been a Westwood officer shot in Williamson's time with the department, but several years ago, an Idaho Trooper had been killed during a routine traffic stop along State Highway 95 near Athol. The Trooper, David Lorenz, bled out while waiting for an ambulance, but his last words into his radio, "Shots Fired! Officer Down!" got the attention of every law enforcement officer in a fifty-mile radius. If you had a badge, a gun, took an oath to defend the public, and one of your brothers had been shot, you would drop everything to catch the motherfucker that did it.

The dispatcher at the Kootenai County Emergency Center did a fantastic job relaying information to the parties joining the search, including the location of the initial stop, the last known direction, a vehicle description, and the registered owner of the stopped vehicle. The radio traffic was chaotic until a voice announced that Trooper Lorenz was 10-42, End of Watch, dead. At that point, in the radio's silence, you could feel the group of cops take a deep breath and reassert their efforts to find the offender.

A State Fish and Game officer and a Boundary County deputy encountered the car and the suspect outside Moyie Springs as he tried to enter Montana. The suspect in the smaller Ford sedan was no match for the Fish and Game officer's faster and heavier Ford F250, which applied a PIT technique where the pursuing vehicle pressed its front fender to the rear corner of the suspect vehicle and gave it a swift turn. If done smoothly, and in this case, it was, this would cause a spin-out of the target.

The Boundary County deputy was ready. When the sedan spun into the gravel on the shoulder, he parked his Explorer nose-to-nose with it, blocking any chance of escape. The suspect's chance for freedom was on foot, and only with two other officers in the way of it. It didn't end well. By the time he exited his vehicle with his gun in his hand, the two cops were already in position to defend themselves and weren't in the mood to be overly lenient, seeing as this man had killed one of their brothers.

There was palpable relief on the radio when Deputy Aaron Leinhart of Boundary County said, "Suspect 10-7. We're good."

Across Kootenai County, law enforcement officers hoped for a similar message of good news about Husted, but as Williamson monitored the radio chatter, he knew that message would never come.

56

I knew I was back in cell range when my phone dinged with notifications. There were four texts from the chief.

Come to the station.

Hey!

Where are you?

And the last …

Never mind. We may have found Husted.

That last one was a pleasant surprise. I still had too little information to know how Husted and Gillum's disappearance worked into the mix. What I did know was that Williamson was behind it. I knew he was a bad cop, a killer, and most likely a drug runner of some kind. I knew the chief and most of the police were busy searching for Husted, and that Williamson seemed to set himself up for some grand departure. I didn't know where Williamson planned to head in this escape, but I knew roughly where the old cop lived, and I wasn't sure how to get there. I headed in that direction, hoping that I'd cross paths. I wasn't sure what to do when I got there, but I'd figure that part out when I needed to.

I grabbed my phone, opened the Google Voice app, and, using the number I'd previously signed up for with fake information, called Kootenai County dispatch on their local line. That line was probably recorded, too, but wouldn't have the same tracking capabilities as the official 911 system.

"County Dispatch." The voice on the phone was calm and clear.

Using a flat affect and a slightly higher pitch in my voice, I said, "A white GMC flatbed truck left Upriver Paper Mill ten minutes ago, heading south on Ninety-five. Two male occupants. On the bed, you'll see three full pallets, but if you search them, you'll find they're hiding a huge load of fentanyl. If you go back to the mill, look in the garage shed. You'll find at least one dead body." I finished the call in less than thirty seconds. I wasn't sure what was in the load, but I knew the "F" word would get all sorts of attention. The troopers wouldn't care as much if a load of marijuana came through, but a huge fentanyl bust would be a boon for any department. Still on my phone, I looked for the best route to Williamson's house and saw it was in a wooded area east of Spirit Lake. Though not far as the crow flies, the number of winding roads made for a longer drive than I would have thought. I eventually made my way to his neighborhood.

I drove past Williamson's cabin slowly to get an idea of the land and saw no neighbors within a mile. Williamson's property seemed big enough, but the extra solitude came from the fact that so few of the parcels had ever been developed. It appeared the old cop had the whole side of the mountain to himself.

57

By the time he turned into his driveway, Williamson had choreographed the next few minutes of his life down to the second. He pulled into his garage. Leaving the bag in the passenger seat, he stepped out and walked over to his workbench to grab a box of matches. From his pockets and gear belt, he pulled out his wallet, two pistols, and Husted's radio, and when sure that he had everything, he stripped naked and put his clothes into the wood stove in the corner. He squirted a healthy stream of lighter fluid inside and touched a lit match to a wet piece of his undershirt. It wasn't long before the mix of kindling, lighter fluid, and cotton teamed up to make a fine blaze. Williamson opened the lower vents to let in more air, which raised the fire's roar and generated even more heat. His heavy Carhartt coat was tough to stuff in, and for a moment, he was worried that he had snuffed the flames out when he used a stick to push the whole thing in. Smoke kept coming; within a minute, Williamson could see flames licking up from the back of the stove.

The warmth felt good on his exposed skin. It was crisp outside, but almost pleasant; still early spring. Not warm enough to lounge about naked, so he enjoyed the fire while it lasted. The coat was in flames and had mostly disappeared, leaving room for his boots. Shoving them into the stove one at a time, he watched as the oil and polish in the leather quickly bubbled out, adding to the light and heat inside. Wolverines; water-repellent Wolverines with enough insulation for chilly, wet days. Boots he loved. He'd have to pick up another pair somewhere along the line.

Once he was sure everything in the stove that needed to go was in, he added several pieces of fir and tamarack and dampened the vents so it would burn slowly and hot inside. Before leaving for good, he'd come and make sure that it was all gone. He went inside to finish his preparations.

Williamson enjoyed his modest home. He had done most of the work himself, except for the concrete foundation and the transport of the shell. He had a friend do the drywall and plaster, but he did everything else. It took longer than planned, and he had been living in a construction zone for a couple of years, but that was long ago. This little corner of the world had served him well. Twenty-some years ago, the owner of this vast plot of land sold it to a hopeful developer who cut it into twenty-acre lots, hoping to sell them off and build homes for the new buyers. It didn't quite work out that way. Any new dwellings built would have to be off-grid for a few years until power, water, or sewer lines were brought in. There was only a small pool of people who wanted that life, loners like Williamson. The developer went bankrupt and ran away from the whole thing within three years. Keeping Husted's police radio turned on and in hand, he strode naked through his kitchen and living room, heading directly for the bathroom for a quick, hot shower, content with the developer's poor choices that had left Williamson without neighbors. Without witnesses.

58

A half-mile past the house and uphill, I turned the car around and headed back down, stopping around a bend 200 feet from the entrance of the house's driveway. The trees here were pine, like back at the mill, but they were all taller, like someone had cleared the forest of smaller trees, leaving the big ones. Not at all uncommon. It was a sensible way to clear the forest floor of deadwood and made for a prettier view.

That clarity wasn't helpful to me as I carefully made my way toward the cabin. He had probably brought the simple, manufactured house to the site in pieces and had it assembled atop a concrete foundation. It had no garden or traditional yard space of any kind, and the woods came directly up to the perimeter of the foundation, with clumps of ninebark, hawthorn, and Rocky Mountain maple scattered about wherever the randomness of nature decreed or wherever Williamson allowed them to stay.

I moved to a shady clump near the driveway, about 100 feet from the front porch. Fifty feet to the cabin's east and across the gravel lot stood a two-car garage, a pole barn like mine but a much smaller version. The main garage door was open, and I could see Mallard's Jeep inside. Smoke rose from a vent on the roof. As my eyes adjusted to the darkness inside the garage, I saw an old-style pot-bellied stove in the corner and, through the vents in the front, the last flames of a fire.

Now what? I thought. Another treeline and another shady clump of shrubs. I hadn't planned any further than this. With no clear options, I defaulted to a sensible choice: explore the area without getting seen and figure out the rest as I went.

Though it was midday and the forest was mostly clear, there were enough large groupings of underbrush that I could stay out of sight. First, I moved parallel to the driveway, away from the main house, toward the road. 200 feet further from the house, the driveway made a modest turn, and that's where I crossed to the other side. If Williamson were on the porch looking down the lane, he still wouldn't have seen me.

Once across, I kept heading straight into the woods for as far as I could go while being blocked from view by the garage outbuilding. The hillside continued on a gentle slope downward to the south and west, but I couldn't see any sign of other houses or properties.

I turned right and headed back toward the back of the garage. During occasional stops to listen for sounds from the house, I noted there were no artificial sounds at all. There seemed to be no one close. I had passed few homes along my drive here, and I assumed I might hear a car from the highway down the hill, but there was nothing.

The garage had a door on its western wall that faced the house, but I knew it was open. I stayed close to the eastern wall and approached the driveway again. I remembered the vehicle's basic layout relative to the wall and was sure I could get between them.

I hurried into the garage and avoided tripping over the long-handled yard tools leaning against the wall.

After touching the engine block to confirm it was still warm, I moved over to the woodstove and workbench.

I saw it. I saw them: a Glock, the suppressed .22, and a police radio. Last, I took a quick peek inside Williamson's vehicle and saw the black bag. Before I even opened it, I knew what I'd find inside.

59

The shower reinvigorated him so much that Williamson didn't regret that it threw him off track by a few minutes. Stepping out of the stall, the first thing he did was check the time on his phone and see if there had been any further attempts to call him in to help with the search. Nothing. That was mainly good, but he hoped the chief wouldn't send a car out to check on him. The odds of that were slim, though. He lived a good bit out of town and assumed that all available bodies were on the road heading to the southwest corner of the county to look for Husted near the Speedway. The radio chatter indicated extra activity because of a big traffic stop, but he couldn't discern all the details. It sounded south of him, so he wasn't too worried about it. He was headed north.

Naked, he went to the spare bedroom and withdrew two large canvas duffel bags from the closet. He had already calculated what he could bring now and what he'd need to buy or scrounge along the way. From the same closet, he grabbed several of his sweaters, neoprene long johns, and at least a dozen pairs of socks he wore while hunting or hiking. He stuffed those items into one of the canvas bags, and before leaving the room, he grabbed two parkas hanging on the rack. One was a thick, thigh-length coat that could take the worst of the Inland Northwest winter, and the other would keep him dry and warm through the worst monsoon or the wetness of a spring thaw. That's all he needed from here.

In the closet of his bedroom, he grabbed two handfuls of shirts from the rod and two sweaters from there. From the dresser, he took two handfuls of underwear and an equal number of black socks from the next drawer down. In the drawer next to them were the T-shirts. Williamson grabbed them all and stuffed them into the bags with all the other goodies.

From the top shelf of the closet, he grabbed a smaller canvas bag and headed back into the bathroom. From the medicine cabinet, he grabbed only the toiletries he'd need in the near future, as well as his prescription medications and a spare pair of eyeglasses. Grabbing a few items from the shower, he headed back into his room, stopping at the linen closet in the hallway to grab three towels.

Still naked, he stood in his room and paused. *What else?* The battle between fatigue and excitement had his head spinning. He had to calm himself as he got dressed. Dressing allowed him time to go over what else he might need to grab, and once he had tightened the laces of his second favorite pair of boots, he was back on mental track. He stood up and headed to his office.

There, he took a few moments to clear several items on his laptop before detaching the external hard drive. That he put to the side. He grabbed the laptop and cracked it against his knee, snapping it in two with a lot of crumbs. In the rubble in his right hand, he dug through the remnants until he found the SSD drive. He took it and put it on top of the hard drive. From the bottom drawer of the desk, he grabbed a collection of

275

folders held together by a rubber band, and beneath them were two passports: one U.S. and the other Canadian. Lastly, he grabbed a large envelope that was tucked in the drawer. Inside it, $40,000 in cash. His escape fund. Paltry when compared to what he had in the black bag, but it would still be handy to have.

Williamson grabbed the lot and returned to his bedroom, where he stuffed the new items into one of the canvas bags. With a few more odds and ends grabbed, he was ready to go. His guns and camping gear were in the garage, so he could load those things after he put the canvas duffel bags in the Jeep. He'd come back to the house to pack some food for the road, and then he'd have a big decision to make: light the house on fire or not.

He really liked his house, but that wasn't the issue. Williamson was toying with the idea of making it look as if someone had taken him, like Gillum or Husted. If he didn't burn it and disappeared, the Troopers or Feds could tell he went away on his own. He was sure he'd covered his tracks well enough, but knowing they were looking was worrisome. If they thought he was dead, it might alter the way they searched for him. As he covered the distance between his porch and the back of the Jeep, his mind turned to thoughts of food. He hadn't eaten all day, and his body was letting him know it.

He set the bags down near the Jeep's rear bumper and opened the hatch using the handle. Reaching down and lifting the two bags into the rear, he felt they must have gotten heavier in the few seconds they were on the ground. That, or he really needed some food. Walking around the Jeep to the workbench, he intended to grab some camping gear from the high shelf above it. He saw Husted's radio and Glock, but the suppressed .22 was missing.

He barely had time to register that when a voice called out from behind him.

"Hey!"

Williamson turned his head around and felt the blood fall from his face as he saw Karl Warren staring him down with his .22 pointed toward him.

60

Two Years Earlier

"So how much cash are we talkin' about?" Doc Bradley asked. He leaned forward in his expensive leather chair onto his expensive mahogany desk in his spacious office in his too-expensive building. Doc had extended all his credit to set himself up as a successful attorney and was hoping to all the gods that it would help bring in clients.

"None!" Warren replied curtly but with a slight, embarrassed smile. "We're talking only about theoretical money here."

"Okay, then. How much theoretical cash are we talkin' about?" Doc understood the distinction and knew what Warren was getting at.

Warren took a moment to reflect on whether he really wanted to tell anyone. He sipped his bourbon to kill another thirty seconds, but finally let it out, deciding that he needed the help. "Just under two point four million. Mostly hundreds, but a few bundles of twenties thrown in."

Doc paused again, taking a sip of his own drink. Warren could see the wheels turning in the lawyer's mind, weighing the various ways to make cash disappear. Doc Bradley, known in the real world as Douglas Bradley, was a newly minted attorney in Missouri specializing in family law and personal finance. Those areas of specialization were only part of why Warren chose Bradley to chat with. Mostly, it was because of their shared history.

The two were never stationed in the same unit, but they served together in the U.S. Army. Bradley had been a medic stationed at Ramstein Air Force Base, and Warren was an investigator assigned to USAREUR there. They never worked together, but as things go, when you're in a foreign land doing one's duty, you meet by chance and form a strong comradeship. Shared beer and schnitzel followed, along with war stories and shit-talking. When you meet a kindred spirit, you know it. And both did.

"Well," Doc started, "there are a few ways to go about it. You could keep it all on the DL and live off the cash as you go. You'll have to live a simple life, but it's low-risk. Downside is that you'll always have to have a shitload of cash around you. That can be an upside, too, as you'll have liquidity that can't be traced." After a pause, Bradley asked, "Can I ask where this theoretical money came from?"

"I found it," Warren said in a manner that invited no follow-up questions. Doc wanted to know more, but as they had the beginning of an attorney-client relationship, it was better not to follow up yet.

"Okay, for now. Knowing you," Doc said, "you won't want to live a flashy lifestyle anyway. I assume you're good with that. I'd say cash out your 401 (k) or IRAs, take the tax hit, and buy some property. Flip it and exaggerate the cash income. Take that tax hit, too. You'd need to find a borderline-reputable attorney who knows property law. I know a guy. In fact, I am that guy."

Doc paused and looked off in the distance. He leaned back in his leather chair and chewed on his pen, the mocha skin highlighting the perfect American mix of the black and brown ethnicities that get the fewest opportunities in life, mixed with a random European down the line somewhere. He once said he was the best and the worst that the country had to offer. In his three generations past, his family tree had covered all the ethnic bases to the point where everyone excluded them. Too black, not brown enough, too brown, not white enough. In his youth, Doc said, "Fuck it!" joined the U.S. Army, ate shit for a while, but put himself through law school using the government's money, and made his own way, taking care of family as he went.

His wheels were turning, picking up new ideas, reviewing them, then discarding them if they didn't fit. "Yeah. Rental properties. That's your best bet. Start an LLC and flip a few shitty houses. Work your way up from shitholes to decent pieces. Overstate your cash expenses, overstate any cash income, pay for everything from your business accounts, and make as many purchases as possible under the business name. Pay taxes on everything, even when you think you can fudge some income. Don't."

Maybe it was the bourbon, or the realization that he might have found an escape from this life, but Warren was calmer and more content than he had been in months.

61

Finding live weapons lying about the garage increased my sense of anxiety. I sure as hell didn't want to get trapped in here if Williamson came out, so I had to move fast. I assumed that the old cop was preparing to get out of the area for good and wouldn't let an ex-cop like me get in the way, so I had to act quickly to implement my hasty plan.

From the table, I grabbed the Glock and did what I always did with every single unattended weapon I'd ever encountered: I cleared it. With the pistol in my right hand, I dropped the magazine and set it on the workbench. Next, I rotated the weapon counterclockwise and covered the ejection port with my left hand. Using my left thumb and forefinger, I slid the upper receiver of the pistol to the rear and caught the ejected round in my left palm. I set the round down next to the magazine and promptly emptied it. I grabbed a rag from the bench, wiped every part of the weapon, and put it back together with the empty magazine—the rounds I placed into my pocket for now. I gave the weapon a final wipe down and set it back on the bench.

I grabbed the .22 and performed a similar clearing action. This time, though, after clearing it and wiping my prints from the ejected round, I reloaded it correctly and kept it with me. Last, I secured the black bag and headed out the garage door. Before coming into sight, I took a glance toward the house, and when it was clear and quiet, I headed back around the Jeep and toward the outside of the eastern wall of the garage.

I waited. I knew Williamson would soon come to the garage, then go deeper into it to retrieve his things from the bench. Then, I'd have Williamson trapped in the spot I had wanted to avoid.

It was four minutes before Williamson left through the front door and headed toward the Jeep. By sound alone, I could track him. I needed Williamson to go into the garage without giving him enough time to grab the other pistol. Williamson made a slight grunt when he hoisted the bags into the Jeep, and the footsteps moved toward the workbench.

Now!

I left my position and made a modest arc outward toward the open garage door. Not enough distance to be a problem if I had to shoot, but with enough extra space to move laterally if Williamson had another weapon I hadn't counted on. Nothing. I saw the man's empty hands, came closer, and announced myself.

"Hey!"

Williamson's body stopped, and his head turned slowly to lock eyes with me, but only after he saw that I had his pistol pointed at him.

"Keep your hands out. Turn around toward me," I said. As the old cop turned, I saw his eyes shift to the weapon. Good. Williamson knew it was there and how far away it was. Once we were facing each other, I began my rehearsed presentation.

"I have a choice to make. The first option is simply to kill you, take the money, and hide the evidence. The other option, and this is where your cooperation will come in helpful, is to take half the money and let you run away. If you run and hide as you intended, you'll have the Feds after you. That surely helps me out by keeping the focus on you. I assume you've got plans for what you'll do, and I assume you've thought it through, so I won't worry too much about you. You know that if I were committed to the first option, you'd be dead already. If I just wanted to turn you in, I'd have made the call already."

"Sure," Williamson said.

Warren began again. "Tell me a few things. Are Gillum and Husted dead?"

A long pause, but Williamson weighed the odds and eventually spoke. "Yes."

"Correct me if I say something wrong here." I needed more information before I made my decision. "You and Mallard ran a transfer point for drugs from Canada. You'd hold it and hand it off to the next round of goons. Those goons would pay you, you'd take your cut and send the rest of the money back north. Good so far?"

Just a nod from Williamson.

"Me finding the bodies brought a lot of attention to Baker and the mill. Gillum was getting scared and stupid, and you wanted to eliminate that problem before it messed up today's transfer. Husted was an accident, and once you killed him, you realized that your time here was at an end. That's why your exit plan seems rushed. Close?"

A shrug from Williamson. "Yeah. Pretty good."

"I don't care about Gillum, but where's Husted's body at?"

Another shrug from Williamson. This one, though, was more of an "I don't know" shrug. "By now," he said, "there probably isn't a body anymore. Within a week or so, what's left will be spread throughout the county. You'll never find anything."

I wasn't sure what that meant, but small details like that didn't seem paramount right now. The cop was dead, and he was never coming back. "How much is in the bag? It seems like a lot, but I didn't have time to count."

I could see Williamson weighing whether to tell the truth, and I tried to imagine how he might think in that position. A good lie might give him a few more minutes to figure out what to do. Sure, I might let him go with half of the cash, but if the roles were reversed, he wouldn't hesitate to get me out of the way. Would a higher number make me more likely to share the money, or would it inspire greed? Would a lower number make me think that the whole mess wasn't worth it? Would I kill him and take it all, or turn him in? He could go to prison if he had to. He must have enough connections in the militias and white power movements that he could survive prison, but the bigger reality was that I would just end it all here and now.

"Just over three million." There was almost an audible hint of pain in Williamson's voice when he said that because he knew there was slim chance he was getting out of here with that much, even if I were generous. "What do you want to do, Warren?"

Decision time. I hoped to get a location for Husted's body, but that didn't look like it would happen. "That pistol you left on the bench is empty now. I was thinking that it might make me feel better if I had to shoot you if you went for it. I don't think we're gonna need that now."

I took two steps backward and quickly glanced down the dirt and gravel driveway to make sure no one had arrived during our time in the garage. Nothing. "Walk toward me," I said to Williamson as he walked backward toward the house. When Williamson was twelve feet outside the garage, I motioned for him to stop.

"Now what?" the old cop said. "What are you doing? What do you want me to do?"

"Nothing," Warren said. "You don't need to do anything."

There was silence as I steeled myself and as Williamson figured out what was about to happen.

As Williamson began a futile rush toward me, two quick spits of noise and smoke came from the suppressed pistol and into Williamson's right knee. The physics of it were quite simple. Though the .22 doesn't have any stopping power to speak of, if you remove the support structure for a 250-pound man, that man will fall in place. Just like a tall pine that has had a good portion of its base whacked away by an ax.

Williamson clutched at his knee and screamed in pain. I stood motionless. "If I were to shoot you in the garage," I began, "I'd have to worry about cleaning up all the blood. Here, it'll get mixed up in the dirt and gravel. The next rain we have, and we've been having a lot of that, will wash away what's left."

From Williamson, nothing. No pleading, yelling, or cursing. Just a look that said, "Go fuck yourself!"

I didn't feel bad as I raised the gun and put three more rounds into his head and face. I knew that there was a severe depression cycle ahead of me when this was done, but I didn't have time for that now. I didn't bother checking for a pulse. Anyone with that many holes in their head won't have much to say anymore. I picked up the spent brass and headed to the garage.

Having almost tripped over the yard tools upon entering the garage, I knew exactly where they were. Before returning to the body, I grabbed a wheelbarrow, a D-nose shovel, a rock rake, a mattock, Husted's radio, and Glock. Williamson hadn't moved. Though I'm strong, moving a body is invariably harder than moving an equivalent amount of iron at the gym. The barbells are evenly weighted and balanced, whereas a dead human flops and slides any way gravity tells it to. Still, I muscled the corpse into the wheelbarrow, stacked the tools, radio, and weapon on top of him, and moved into the woodline.

After a few feet, I stopped and grabbed the rock rake. Returning to where Williamson fell, I raked the soil and gravel until there was no trace of blood left in the driveway.

The land sloped gently downward, with numerous minor humps and ridges. I looked for a low spot that might flood with rain or snowmelt but wouldn't be enough of a downslope to become a small stream in heavy rains. Nearly 200 feet downhill and in the middle of a mixed thicket, I found what I needed. The soil on the hillside was far less rocky than on my bottomland, and the work went quickly with the mattock and shovel. When I found a stone, I'd put it aside for later.

I stopped once, laughing out loud at a thought that I had. Right before I shot him the final three times, I should have said, a la Chief Brody, "Smile, you son of a bitch!" It wasn't really that funny a thought, but the laughter broke some of my tension.

After a furious twenty-five minutes of work, I made the slight depression into a three-foot-deep hole. It wasn't as long as I would have liked, but it'll do. Once satisfied, I unceremoniously dumped Williamson from the wheelbarrow into the hole. I took a minute to position the body so that it would lie as deeply as possible; then, I reached into my pocket for the rag and rounds from the other pistol. One by one, I wiped them clean and tossed them into the hole alongside the body. I did the same with the Glock and police radio.

I could feel my fatigue, but knew the end was near. I placed the stones that I had put aside into the hole first, hoping to make it difficult for coyotes to dig through and pull him out. The dirt went next, and I used the rock rake to smooth the remaining soil as best I could. Next, I scoured the forest floor for as many large branches or downed trees as I could find to place as much debris on the grave as possible.

When I was done, it looked like an innocent thicket of saplings and shrubs filled with loose branches, a wholly natural part of the Idaho landscape. In a few weeks of spring, the shrubs will be thick with new leaves, and the spot very well may go undiscovered.

With a few minutes of replacing the tools in the garage and wiping anything I had handled, the scene looked untouched. I grabbed the bag I had stashed and headed back through the woods for a hike back to my car on the road.

Though only ten or twelve miles from my home on the prairie, this part of the county was in a different climate zone. The elevation kept it colder, and the tall peaks and dense woods kept the place in the shade. Snow lived a much longer life here than on my farm. On the drive back down the mountain, several of the draws in the switchbacks still held thickly packed mounds of snow. In some of these areas, cedars stayed huddled close to the runoff streams and didn't let any of the lesser pines share their space. The pines could grow almost anywhere and had a wide range. The cedars, though, were fussier and had fewer places from which to choose.

Soon, though, the cedars disappeared. Even the pines dwindled away, and I had open valley on either side. Fields of dark soil, fertile with sleeping alfalfa, hay, or buckwheat, sat awaiting the next round of growth, harvest, growth, harvest, and slumber. The midday sun was warm, at least for Idaho this time of year, so I rolled the window down and right away heard the hum of the power lines overhead. A barely audible tone, more felt than heard. An oddly comforting sound and feel. It seemed a warm welcome on my way back to my dirt and my girls.

62 - Sunday

Big Red set the world in motion with his first call of the morning. It was a few minutes earlier than I had planned to get up, but there was no going back to sleep once the king began his crowing. I checked the clock: 5:22. Not bad. After a good stretch and scratch, I pulled myself out of my warm bed and headed to the kitchen. I had the timer on the coffee machine for 5:30, but I pressed the start button so I wouldn't have to wait.

I grabbed a hoodie and slipped into my garden clogs, then stepped into my garden to let the girls out for the day. In the east, the barest hint of dawn poked above the mountains and forests, while a trace of frost on the ground caught the light's sparkle. When the girls heard my footsteps, their clamor and excitement grew, but they didn't escape when I opened the outer door. As always, they walked in a tight group around me as I went for the feed bag and the magical red bucket. I had to brush one girl off the bin lid after she had jumped up there when I opened it.

"Good girl," I said as she fluttered off and away.

They went where the bucket went, and it went, in my hand, out to the compost box. I had placed some kitchen scraps in there last night, and the girls who saw them made quick work of them as they tore through the garden waste to find the newly strewn beans, too. I tossed the red bucket toward the coop but headed out to the overgrown grasses near the border of my property and the goat pen. Sanchez's team took good care of my girls, and I didn't lose any hens to predators while I was gone, but I would remain vigilant in my habit of peeing in the field at various points to make sure that the other critters would know an alpha predator was living here again.

The coffee should be ready now, so I finished my business, took a few minutes to gather the eggs from the previous night, and headed in for a cuppa. The smell of the brew left a strong impression and made me happier the moment I caught a whiff of it in my home. Warm and reassuring, almost as if the past few days hadn't been littered with death and misery. The warmth of the moment brought me back to reality, and the weight of events slowed me, making me feel heavy. Filling my mug, I stepped onto the front porch and made myself comfortable in an Adirondack chair to greet the day. Hopefully, it would be a day with as little human interaction as possible. This mess had drained my batteries and soul more than I had thought, wearing me down both by the misdeeds of others and by the weight of shame for my actions. In time, I knew I'd be okay with my decision to kill and bury Williamson, and I'd make some good come from the new cash. Husted's family may want some closure for their loss, but I didn't know where the body was. Making sure that the cop killer was dead was as much as I could do for the family.

Yesterday, Sanchez said she'd get an update from Fuller later that night and would be sure to share what she could. *It'd be nice if those girls could be identified so their families could rest,* I thought to myself. Selfishly, I supposed that the more girls the authorities identified, there'd be fewer ghosts hanging around this farm, fewer whispers of death.

How could I make peace with this town? How do we forgive people who knew something was amiss but let it slide for so long? Williamson had deep roots in the town, and others must have known what he, Mallard, and Gillum were doing at the mill. Was this small town as full of evil and blindness as Kansas City? What made me think that salvaging twenty acres of dirt and a few birds would help me find peace and ease in this world?

I sat for a few more minutes, then rose before the sun fully crossed the horizon. My coffee, untouched, had gone cold, so I splashed it on the gravel of the yard. Thinking I had thrown more food, several of the girls came over to scratch and peck at the wet spots where the coffee landed. The weight of the world had already drained me, despite the short time I'd been awake. I longed for a nap to improve my mood. The flannel sheets welcomed and comforted me like a parent would a lost child.

Close to 9:30, a text from Sanchez woke me.

You home?

Yes. What's up?

I'll be there in 10.

She was probably the only human I could tolerate today. I got up and made ready for her arrival. Clothed and with teeth brushed, I was on the porch with a cuppa, black, for the Chief as she pulled in.

"Mornin', Chief." I extended the mug. "What you up to today?" I said it cheerfully, but regretted it the moment I remembered she still had an officer missing.

Sanchez caught the tone but ignored it. "I just came back from visiting Lana Goodson. We're sure it was her daughter in the field."

For a full minute, the only response to that news was the sounds of the breeze and the chickens in the yard.

"How many total?" I'd been wanting to know this more than anything. That and how many were identified. I knew that if a body were found and left unnamed, her ghost would stay around the farm, waiting, watching.

"Ten. Three identified. We pulled a lot of personal items from the barn. We'll figure it out soon enough. One of the girls was from Montana, so this is all federal now, or at least out of my hands. Everything we have is going either to the state lab in Moscow or wherever the FBI wants it to go."

More silence, but on the prairie, it's never really silent. Here, the chickens always cluck and hum, and the wind whistles, but there are other sounds. There were birds in the field singing their songs, and you could catch the screech of an owl or a falcon if you were lucky. A football field away, a red-tailed hawk perched on the top of the telephone pole that ran along the road.

I recalled something Trapper Dan had said the first night I had met him at the bar. "Yeah, rabbits are cute, and deer and elk can be majestic, but when push comes to shove, would you rather be a predator or prey?"

I'd been acting like prey for the past year or so. Sure, I'd helped with this mess, but I fell into it. I didn't seek it out. Could I live the rest of my life just enjoying this dirt, or would I have to do something about it, about life and living? On cue, the hawk dove off its perch, swooped low to the ground, and pounced on a field mouse that was going about its day, minding its own mouse business. Better to be the predator in that situation.

"State troopers made a huge drug bust yesterday." Sanchez broke the silence. "County dispatch got an anonymous call about a delivery leaving Upriver Mill, pulled over a transport truck, and found a shitload of drugs. They're still counting, but last I heard, it was a couple of hundred pounds of fentanyl, heroin, and other assorted goodies. They went to the mill and found Williamson's truck, but no sign of him or anyone else. They're still working on a search warrant, but no one can get hold of the owner. It's a shitshow. The local media is going wild with speculation. Huge drug bust, missing cops, missing mill owner. We'll be digging out from under this one for a while."

I nodded without looking at the chief. "That explains what the transfer was all about." I was surprised that they hadn't found Mallard. I had seen him get shot and dragged into the shed. What happened to him after that is one more mystery.

"You know anything about that call?" she asked, but I'm sure she already suspected the answer. The honk of Canada Geese sounded from Radiant Lake. "No, ma'am." A lie. A lie to my best friend, but nothing compared to all the things I won't ever say about yesterday's events.

She paused and looked away. "Didn't think so." She rose from her chair without notice.

"I gotta get back. You'll probably never get back anything we took from your barn, so I hope you weren't attached to it. That little ginger fuck Husted is still missing. We've widened the net and put the word out everywhere, but we're still looking at every road and trail possible. I may grab a four-wheeler and search the trails along the base of Mount Westwood." I was abnormally silent, and it worried her. "You gonna be okay?"

"Yeah," I said slowly. "I'm just in a cocoon mood. Ya know. Just ..." My words trailed off, and I pointed with my thumb over my shoulder. She knew what I meant. I meant that there had been too many dead people in my field and that my brain was too active, and I was doing anything I could to quiet it and keep it that way.

She stood. "Alright, Partner. I'm out. Let me know if you need anything." She left with another mug.

I raised mine. "Hoo-uh. Stay safe, friend." Her cruiser kicked up a modest dust trail as she headed back to town, and for a few moments, the sound of her tires on gravel covered up the sounds of the prairie, but as she got further away, the nature song returned and got louder.

In the mixed flock of hens, the five Rhode Island Reds always stuck together, usually moving in a line to corral any bugs that might be in their path. If a cricket jumped out of the way of one gal, it went right into the path of another—teamwork at its best. The girls had been making their way toward the porch. When they noticed me, they came closer, hoping that, somehow, the magical red bucket of goodness would appear and that divine seeds and beans would come their way. No such luck this morning. Sometimes, I would get them an extra scoop because watching them was so enjoyable and comforting. Instead, I looked at them as they looked at me and asked them for some advice.

"Well, girls—now what?"

When no pearls of wisdom came forth, I got up from the chair and headed for the barn. I needed to finish what I had started last week. There were more stones to harvest.

About the Author

Daniel D. Baumer served in the U.S. Army and was a law enforcement officer. He is the author of *The Stone Harvest*, the first in the Karl Warren series, and its follow-up, *Deadlined*. His stories are inspired by his life experiences and the people he has encountered in his many travels and adventures. Learn more about him at danieldbaumer.com.

www.ingramcontent.com/pod-product-compliance
Lightning Source LLC
Chambersburg PA
CBHW070759280326
41934CB00012B/2983